# Next Foot Forward

*By*
*Adelina Basile*

**Adelina Basile**

Copyright © 2025 Adelina Basile

All rights reserved.

No part of this publication may be reproduced, stored in a retrieval system, or transmitted in any form or by any means, electronic, mechanical, photocopying, recording or otherwise, without the prior written permission of the copyright owner, except for brief quotations used in reviews or academic work.

**Next Foot Forward**

*For my sons*

Adelina Basile

# About the Author

*Adelina Basile is a poet, artist, and advocate whose work transforms personal pain into public healing. She lives on bushland in NSW, where she raises animals, grows food, and writes barefoot.*

## Acknowledgment

*I respectfully acknowledge the Biripi people, Traditional Custodians of the land where this book was written. I honour their Elders past and present, and the rich cultural heritage that continues to shape this country.*

Adelina Basile

# Table of Content

About the Author ............................................................................... iv

Acknowledgment ................................................................................ v

Chapter 1 ............................................................................................. 9

Chapter 2 ........................................................................................... 11

Chapter 3 ........................................................................................... 13

Chapter 4 ........................................................................................... 17

Chapter 5 ........................................................................................... 20

Chapter 6 ........................................................................................... 26

Chapter 7 ........................................................................................... 31

Chapter 8 ........................................................................................... 33

Chapter 9 ........................................................................................... 37

Chapter 10 ......................................................................................... 46

Chapter 11 ......................................................................................... 56

Chapter 12 ......................................................................................... 61

Chapter 13 ......................................................................................... 68

Chapter 14 ......................................................................................... 73

Chapter 15 ......................................................................................... 76

Chapter 16 ......................................................................................... 81

Chapter 17 ......................................................................................... 83

Chapter 18 ......................................................................................... 88

Chapter 19 ......................................................................................... 91

Chapter 20 ......................................................................................... 98

## Next Foot Forward

| | |
|---|---|
| Chapter 21 | 102 |
| Chapter 22 | 106 |
| Chapter 23 | 107 |
| Chapter 24 | 109 |
| Chapter 25 | 111 |
| Chapter 26 | 120 |
| Chapter 27 | 122 |
| Chapter 28 | 127 |
| Chapter 29 | 129 |
| Chapter 30 | 134 |
| Chapter 31 | 139 |
| Chapter 32 | 149 |
| Chapter 33 | 153 |
| Chapter 34 | 159 |
| Chapter 35 | 161 |
| Chapter 36 | 163 |
| Chapter 37 | 165 |
| Chapter 38 | 168 |
| Chapter 39 | 172 |
| Chapter 40 | 175 |
| Chapter 41 | 181 |

**Adelina Basile**

*I pass this story on as someone who's lived with autism and PTSD; memories may be affected by dissociation, and I hope you will read them with patience and care.*

Next Foot Forward

# Chapter 1

"Float back," said my therapist. "Surround yourself with the trees, ocean, rocks and all those guiding figures that have kept you safe. Lina. You have lived a life surrounded by incredible guardians."

"Think about it. Every tree you have sat under, every rock you have climbed. The sky above and the moon that lights the night. They have watched over you. They have kept you safe and given you a powerful belonging."

"Trust them. Visit your memories knowing they are holding you."

I lie against the warm rock and let the sun touch my skin, while the salt hanging on the wind finds my face and hair. I lick it with my tongue and taste my childhood, my peaceful life, once again. My heart beats to the rhythm of the waves as they scrunch themselves on the shore.

My family spent half of each year at this tiny cove, and it feels as safe to me now as it was all those years ago. It is early autumn, my favourite season. This is the village of my birth. This mid-north coastal area of NSW held fertile dairy pasture from the turn of the twentieth century until the mid-seventies. Milk, cream and bread were delivered to our small houses in the past. The land is now abandoned by farmers and sweeps down gentle hills and scrubby bush to the seashore. Endless screaming southerlies have forced dwellers further inland, but the churning agitation of my ocean calls to me as it calls the gulls and pied oystercatchers, sea eagles and all things winged and finned.

I can follow my own two-year-old footprints around the rocks and crouch in the small caves where I used to spend hours. Curled inside my stony hideout, I would watch the crabs as they madly semaphored with their front legs, making themselves look important. This was the only place in the world where I was me. If I possessed the olfactory sense of my dog, I would be able to

## Adelina Basile

smell my toddler self or find my ladies' Seiko dive watch with the orange band somewhere under this umber-coloured sand. Perhaps even my mother's lost engagement ring that we searched for on our hands and knees when we were all single-digit kids!

One summer my mother's engagement ring was lost on this beach. It was a solitaire diamond that my father took seven years to pay off! My two brothers and I had to crawl through and sift the sand of what felt like a thousand acres. We did that until it was too dark to see, before being called into the house where my father made my mother a sherry to calm her down.

We spent every weekend and school holiday at this beach. My father would catch the school bus and go into Taree where he was the chief linotypist for the Saxby family's *Manning River Times* newspaper.

Remembering my therapist's words to take time to feel secure as I await memories to resurface, I lean back against the cooling dune, close my eyes and listen to this world. The wind has slowed, and the ocean surface has begun rocking gently, waveless, like a boiled pudding on a simmer! The air and sea have made a deal to soothe the sweet Pacific.

Awareness is everywhere... in the raindrops on the dripping foliage of the wattle trees and in the memory of the soft-shelled crab awaiting his new carapace.

Awareness is everywhere and becomes tangible. There is the scent of the wet, burnt eucalypts hanging in the air... hanging like that dream I failed to remember even though I thought I had.

## Chapter 2

Here I am, decades later, and now trying to satisfy the demands of my therapist. Once more back on my childhood beach, hoping to enjoy or discover some lost memories from my life, memories that had somehow turned into dust and floated off.

Once, this piece of coastal strip had been one great rolling dairy farm parading beside the yellow sand and vast ocean all the way up the coast. Our parents told us that after World War Two, if the farmer liked you, he would sell you a piece of land. Today it is still obvious, as you look at the strange shapes of our yards, that this village, Black Head, had grown in a random manner. If you gathered a hundred dice in your hands, swung around wildly and tossed them, then took note of their landing, you would have achieved similar results to our town planning.

I still live in this village, now abandoned by fishermen and the guesthouse for single men. I retain one of the tiny hardwood shacks, while around me are mostly empty investment houses which only really came alive for a short time in the Covid-19 lockdown, when people were desperate to escape the city.

No one knows where the blocks begin or bleed into each other. Mine's a rectangle, flanked by two triangles that jut out like elbows into the scrub. Two doors up, a house starts as a rectangle, cinches at the waist like a corset, then flares out into a square. The geometry of ownership, odd, silent, precise.

Most houses sit hollow. City folk buy them, knock down the old fibro shacks, and raise concrete fortresses with balconies that stare out to sea. They come for long weekends, fret over salt crusting their windows and seagrass tangling at the shoreline, then vanish. Last night, I walked the dogs through our three streets. Five houses glowed. The rest loomed, dark hulks, probably stuffed with four bedrooms and a media room apiece.

**Adelina Basile**

The air was sharp with salt and the acrid musk of flying foxes, grey-headed, endangered, sweeping overhead in slow, leathery arcs. I like their smell. It clings to the night like burnt eucalyptus. Somewhere above, an owl sliced past my cheek, so close I felt the wind of its wings before I saw it. Silent as a tomb, it vanished into the canopy.

Beneath it all, the waves murmured, low, steady, like breath in the chest of the earth. That sound anchors me. It's the pulse I trust when everything else feels borrowed or broken.

We have a post office and a shop. The town's a thirty-minute drive now. When we were kids, it took longer, an hour sometimes, if a tree had fallen across the dirt track, or if one of us had thrown up from car sickness. The road was red and rutted, and the bush leaned in close, like it wanted to keep us.

Our father was a woeful driver and bought a second-hand Dodge from a retired doctor. He never did bother to get a licence for the first ten years. He had been known to drive the whole thirty miles from beach to town in first gear! My parents both worked in the town and during the school semesters we lived in a high-ceilinged, many-roomed house close to our primary school and church in the town of Taree.

Nature is my salve, my healer and dream-maker. Specifically, this curve of bright sand, the wattle trees and heath plants behind the dune, and the soft but urgent cries of the gulls and terns that hover on the edge of the shoreline, like tiny little trains. Together they are my friends and form the soundtrack of my beach.

Next Foot Forward

# Chapter 3

My father was a linotypist who excelled at his job and almost singlehandedly set out our local paper, the Manning River Times, for printing, four days a week, I think. He sat at a huge machine that cast molten metal as he was typing. His machine was near a window that was always open. After school we could poke our heads in and ask him to make our names. The silver lead with our back-to-front names came into our hands boiling hot. Off we would go, finding mud or ink, chalk or anything that would let us press our names in Times New Roman font. He was an exceptional speller despite leaving school when he was eleven. His first job, after his father was killed accidentally, was as a copy boy for Banjo Paterson, one of Australia's most loved poets and journalists. I know, personally, straight from my father's mouth, that Mr Paterson would send my father out to buy a buttered sweet finger bun every day at around eleven o'clock. Since a young age, my father had smelled of printer's ink and today, that tarry smell takes me back into his after-work cuddle.

Being Italian/Irish, we were Catholic. By the time I was six years old, I knew every Latin word of the Mass. Everything about the church excited my senses. The colours of the stained-glass windows depicting Matthew, Mark, Luke and John were so familiar, I felt they were ancestors; the swirling incense, the bells, the gold and silver glittering all over the altar, and the cold smoothness of the marble tabernacle and altar rails. Words like monstrance, chalice and chasuble danced around my teeth and onto my tongue until I smelt glory.

I remember one year, when I was in grade five, I spent my entire lunch sitting in the church watching the imported Italian artist repainting our Stations of the Cross. Balanced high on a scaffold, he created colours before my eyes. Soft pinks, greys and golden lights were unknown to my ten-year-old eyes. Those skies entranced me. The clouds and light told the story of the Way of the Cross. There was no need at all for the figures. He took about three months to complete them, but I was there, eating my pig's trotter, just enjoying the peace inside the church every day. Once, the Sacred Heart on the wall of the little side altar winked at me.

My Irish Nana, a staunch Republican, had a habit of grabbing one of our fingers in her strong, bony ones and then pinching that poor finger until we were on our knees. All the while laughing and twisting, she would say, "Knitch your larks." We still do not know what it meant! She was also very kind. A regal lady with fine silver-grey hair, knotted on top in the day when she was hatless, and plaited each night.

One holiday afternoon, thick with sun and the smell of roasted meats, the front bedroom turned into a battlefield. My brothers, Michael and Philip, were locked in a furious punch-up, all elbows and adrenaline. Michael, wiry and volatile, and Philip, bulkier now, his new mass tipping the scales in his favour. They crashed into the guest room like a squall, limbs flying, curses cutting the air.

I hovered just outside in the hallway, the silent witness to their chaos. It had become a kind of holiday ritual—masculine energy spilling over like boiling water.

And then Nana.

She swept in from behind me with the speed of a hawk and the voice of a storm. "Boys. Stop that now. Michael! You are the eldest. You should know better!"

Michael turned, guilty as a child. But the moment hung too long.

Philip's fist—massive, misdirected, and merciless—hurtled past Michael's shoulder and collided squarely with Nana's temple.

Time stopped.

### Next Foot Forward

She fell without grace, crumpling like a crow hit mid-flight. Silence thudded into the room. My brothers froze, their quarrel vanishing into the shock of what had just happened.

And in that instant, all the strength in the room shattered. I thought they had killed her, and maybe they did too. My brothers did nothing and just stood around her on the floor, speechless and useless. I developed such fear and panic that I vomited and then ran and hid in the broom cupboard. When she did regain her wits, she stood as straight-backed as a broom and said to us, "If any of you tell your parents about this, I will kill you!" The whisker on her chin quivered.

Nana used to come up from Sydney to mind us whenever it was school holidays and we had to be in town. I never once remember her at our beach shack. That was probably because there was only an outside dunny, and we were always told to beware of hookworm. I had two brothers and one sister, and we had freedom to do as we wished. Of course, we had rules like "don't play with matches" and "don't eat green plums," and the most important one of all, "Stay in your own backyard!", but that was about it.

In town, we lived in a street where everyone knew and helped each other. The houses were all on quarter-acre blocks, and most had twelve-foot-high ceilings. This was a timber area, so our fences were all of hardwood, as were most of the houses. At dusk, voices rose like birdsong… Barry calling for his dog, Mrs D laughing at something unseen. The sound drifted through the timber, warm and familiar, like bread baking or rain on a tin roof. And it was comforting to hear those voices. At night we could hear the calls of the tawny frogmouth birds and sometimes, if you went to the outside toilet in the night, you could feel the air move in a wave as a tawny flew past, as silent as death.

Mrs D's arm would appear above the fence line, flinging a bulging grocery bag into our yard—jumpers, pillowcases, sandshoes with the laces knotted together. "Still good," she'd shout, already

## Adelina Basile

halfway back to her laundry. The sandshoes that I was wearing on the day I will tell you of, were in one of her throwaway bags, under some jumpers and pillowcases.

Our street was high up in our friendly small town that had grown along the edge of the river. The river had been explored by Captain William Wynter, who had received a land grant of fertile ground in 1831. The town is on part of that granted land. There were three hotels on the edge of that wide and beautiful river, which was at the bottom of our hill. Houses were on pilings when I was a kid. You could get under and escape from the adult wrath. It is strange how I don't remember being "naughty." Does anyone?

Rain turned the earth to velvet under that house in Wynter Street. I'd crawl under the house, knees caked, and set up my pulley system—string, buckets, a stick for writing orders in the mud. My workers were invisible but loyal. I was the president, and business was booming.

Once, my mother made me take a bag of kittens down and drop them in that river to drown, when I was about seven years old. I cried the whole way down the hill, and the kittens were scrabbling and howling too, but I was very scared of my mother and pretty much did what I was told. Her blazing blue eyes could loosen my bowels. It would have been better to never have a cat, in my opinion.

The sandshoes from the used clothes bag had fitted me, and I was wearing them that day my world changed.

# Chapter 4

Mr A, the neighbour on the other side of our house, always tossed over sugar bags full of pigs' trotters. People were so kind when I think back along my timeline.

My mother was a city woman who had moved to the country to be with her husband, my father, who had suffered a nervous breakdown in the city and had been advised by doctors to move to the country. She was one of four sisters who had been brought up in Sydney. She remembered that her Irish family had owned hotels and racehorses. She recalled walking with her nana down the length of Cleveland Street, collecting rents from all the tenement houses every Saturday morning. Her father was in line to be the next Postmaster General. However, he died of a burst appendix, and the Irish uncles lost the horses and hotels in card games. My nana ended up destitute with four daughters to raise. My mother was thirteen when her father died, and the second youngest. They were a musical family, and each girl played an instrument or two. Poverty must have come hard to them, and particularly to my mother, who had grand ideas and dreams. She played the piano and the mandolin.

Every Sunday afternoon they held musical soirées at my nana's house. Word spread, and musicians would arrive by bus or train and play music along the street until they found my mother's place. The city of Sydney was little more than a village in the first quarter of the twentieth century. My parents met through music. One of the Sunday afternoon music seekers was my father. He lived in Manly, so had crossed the harbour to meet the four daughters who played music. My father and his brother Joseph were renowned as singers, even from a young age. To quote from his notebook of memories: "The parish priest once said that the nine a.m. Sunday Mass was always full to overflowing. Parishioners came to hear the Basile sopranos singing hymns, now

## Adelina Basile

long forgotten." He had an Italian tenor voice, complete with a tear.

His story clutches my heart. He was one of four brothers, sons of an Aeolian father and a Venetian mother. This was unusual, as the north and south Italians practically spat at each other with hate. However, my grandfather was the provender for all the northern beaches of Sydney Harbour and delivered goods by horse and cart.

When my father was twelve, he saw his own father killed when the horse bucked, overturned the cart, and crushed him. His mother's family did not help, and they were taken in by the church. Until the day he died, my father said that without St Vincent de Paul they would have starved. From the age of twelve, he supported his entire family. He was softly spoken and highly intelligent, but fragile.

He fell in love with my mother, and they were engaged for close to seven years because she was living a very social life in Melbourne. She worked for Il Giornale Italiano, a newspaper bringing the news of Italy to Australia. In the 1920s and 1930s, Italian ships came regularly to Port Melbourne. There were many parties, and the Italian uniforms and men were charming.

My parents courted by handwritten letters and the occasional trip back to Sydney by my mother. Sometimes I think that my father may have been like me, no aspirations, no needs beyond food and shelter, and as much time as he wanted to read and think and dream.

Patience was my father's best trait. Early in their marriage his nerves shattered into another nervous breakdown, and they were advised to get out of the city and away from his family, who were everlastingly in need of money from him. My therapist says that trauma and PTSD can be intergenerational, and the trauma of seeing his father killed before his eyes scarred him deeply. My parents must have been so courageous to leave the city and their

## Next Foot Forward

entire families, carving out a new life in what was then quite a rural area. Besides, my father was obviously of Mediterranean descent, and the Manning area of that time was very "white."

Our country kitchen had a fuel stove, which seemed to be kept going most of the day and often into the night. My father chopped wood, and my two brothers used to split it, as we had both a fuel stove and a fireplace in the lounge room. There was no electric stove, nor hot water. Luckily, Mr A's pigs' feet cooked nicely on a slow fuel stove, and I grew to love them. The girls at school had white bread sandwiches with strawberry jam inside. We never, ever had white bread. My lunch was a cold pig's trotter, gelatinous and yummy. Sometimes, after my mother had opened her shop, she would go to Sydney on stock-buying trips and bring back some delicious salamis and smoked fish roe. I am convinced pigs' trotters are the reason I have such strong fingernails, which I am forever cutting.

Time is like my life's river, and just finding where I am in the story of my life is a great thing. I am on a paddleboard, searching for the special places that held me when I was younger. Youth is supposed to be awkward and clumsy, but sometimes mine was somewhat demented. My wonderful therapist tells me I should lighten my story with some of my poetry, and so I shall leave my memories and sit in the present.

# Chapter 5

These are the 2024 autumn evenings lapping at my feet as I wander through black, moonless nights, remembering a moon on the sea of another place... moons on seas, clichés yet eternally true. Evocative moons call me. The tides are my children. Hints and hues, saturations of tiny pieces of a life half-forgotten, in full colour and motion, surround me like kelp waving under a glassy sea.

In my tattered hope, I stride restlessly forward with a querying eye into my then- and soon-self. The spirits and demons, restless with longing for recognition, cloud and crowd in great comfortability, secure in my essence. I cannot remember ever being comfortable around groups of people. I had inherited my father's timidity and was always anxious that I might make someone unhappy.

We grew up in the days of "a good belting never did harm," and my mother was quick to anger, unreasonably so. One of my brothers was clumsy and stuttered. I lived with the constant worry that he would get a belting that might shatter him. Mostly, when he was in trouble, I would drag him under our back steps, safely out of the way, and then take the blame myself.

It bewilders me that we were ever in such trouble. Sometimes my mother would say, "Just wait till your father comes home!" He would be greeted at the back steps, told of my crime, then take his coat off and say sternly, "Into the bathroom with you." The bathroom, at the end of our built-in verandah, had a floor of strange red concrete. A big claw-foot bath with a chip heater on the tap end of the wall filled one side. Before we could bathe, we had to go gathering chips and sticks. It terrified me, because as the little fire heated the water it came out spitting and snarling, sometimes breathless, like a liquid snake, always boiling hot. On the other wall hung a hook rack with towels and my father's razor strop. Putting his fingers to his lips, he would grin and whisper, "When I hit the bath, you yell." That was how I got belted by my

## Next Foot Forward

father. His eyes were liquid brown with caramel flecks that shot kindness into you. Although he spoke perfect English, he had grown up in a house where Italian was spoken and never could make the "H" sound in front of a word. "House" became "'ouse." A gentle, sometimes feathery voice totally belied the gloriousness of his voice when he sang.

Our backyard was a half-acre of brazen undergrowth, lush green lawn, and a chaotic conglomeration of orchard, fowl yard, duck yard, and two decrepit buildings known fondly as "the old stable" and "the fernery."

The latter, a wobbly wooden trellis, slewed precariously towards the south wall of the house. Its desperate angle screamed "help! I can't," as it stoically supported a gigantic grapevine which flourished in wild abandon and cheerfully dropped bunches of huge purple grapes onto the cracked concrete path below. In summer, our bare feet squished those Isabella grapes with much delight.

A climbing trumpet vine, its flowers vibrantly orange, attracted wasps as well as bees. The shrubs, never pruned or fed, had developed great tangled heads of shiny, thick leaves. Clumps of delicate maidenhair and my mother's potted plants filled the interior of the trellis, creating homes for frogs, spiders, snails, a blue-tongued lizard family, and the resident python.

Each morning, silver threads of snail slime trailed across the jigsaw of broken cement that was the path. Families of noxious weeds claimed survival from the cracks in the path, stubbornly refusing to die despite our attacks with kitchen knives, boiling water, salt, weedkiller and, for a time, heavy plastic which was supposed to cut off the plants' light but ended up tripping us, and tearing.

Between the fernery and the old stable lay the lawn. Always dark green, soft, and fragrantly fresh, it was the accidental result of an unfinished drainage system. Each spring, daffodils, jonquils, and violets poked shy heads through the grass and the air grew heavy with sweetness. Two strange palm trees stood together at the stable entrance. Impossible to climb and good for nothing, they made homes for the stinging hornets... great tall cylinders of grey, towering to ridiculous topknots of spiky fronds.

The stable, a ramshackle old building with a corrugated iron roof, squatted comfortably on rotting foundations. One pane-less window, hung with beautiful cobwebs, let in a stingy ray of light to the deep shadows inside. An old saddle decayed slowly in one corner, and pieces of bridle, girth straps and tarnished bits hung dustily from rusty nails on the wall. An odd assortment of antique furniture, old baby carriages, and broken tools haphazardly filled the remaining space, while a strong smell of mildew drifted through the place.

Bordering the fowl yard was an irregular circle of fruit trees. Never pruned yet always fruitful, they provided a delicious mixture of citrus and stone fruit. The ground beneath was bare dirt, scratched and worn by the mottled collection of crossbred bantams who roosted in the branches of the plum and pear trees.

The ancient mulberry tree stood in the rest of the wild undergrowth. Gnarled boughs spread wide, making comfortable perches for small children, possums, and birds. From the topmost branch I could observe the entire yard and, on a still afternoon, as the sunlight dappled through the flat leaves, the voices of neighbours carried across the tall fences. Clinks of cutlery against china and tempting odours of dinners cooking mingled with the shouts of children's voices, as the soft hues of sunset bathed the garden below in mellow light.

As I rest a while from these childhood memories, I sense a change in the air as I climb back into my now-self. The nor-easterly has pushed past the northern headland, bringing a fresh salty lick to the air. The gulls are sulking; heads tucked behind tightly folded wings as the now fierce nor'easterly rages. The black shag, like a

## Next Foot Forward

sharp and angled monument, squats on his rock with wings stretched wide for feather-drying. A bizarre shape reflected perfectly in the rockpool, like a Japanese ink painting.

My thoughts drift back to the *sumi-e* classes I attended during my years on the island of Okinawa. I treasure my ink stick, so beautifully carved and gilded. A gift from my teacher, of such high quality it made a pure blue-black ink. Kneeling on the soft mats of woven rush (igusa) over rice straw in the *washitsu* (Japanese room) was a reverent act. Before spreading one's rice paper on the felt beneath, it was necessary to sit back on your heels, calm your breathing, and contemplate the brushstroke. Kneeling there in silence, grinding the inkstone, is a precious memory I still cherish.

The sea has given in to the drive and force of the wind. It is now tangled, bursting, and flittering across its own surface, unable to make up its mind. Squinting upwards, my heart lifts in delight, as if someone had cleaned all my blood vessels, because high above, gleeful and proud, rides the juvenile sea eagle, floating and tumbling on thermals. I had watched him fledge two years ago. His flight feathers were not yet as dark or as long as his dad's.

That eagle and I have been acquaintances for about two years now. I have a small, reverent collection of his white underbelly feathers, and several of the long black flight ones too, tokens dropped over time like cryptic offerings. When he passes overhead, his legs gleam, startlingly clean and white, talons half-withdrawn like a predator resting mid-hunt.

Once, while I wandered the beach, wind-whipped and breathless, he soared so low above me I could see the mullet gripped in his claws, its silver body stiff with surrender. The bird relishes my discomfort, I'm sure of it, as the wind snatches my breath and flings coarse, stinging sand at the flesh I cannot conceal. That same flesh, sad to say, once bore the weight of fire.

## Adelina Basile

This communion with nature is what restores me, stitching together time in quiet reverence. But memory pulls me back, to second-hand sandshoes, and the day I was nine and caught fire.

It was the 1950s, Easter school holidays. Our parents were both at work. We four children roamed freely under the loose supervision of our Irish, profoundly deaf Nana. My older brother, newly immersed in physics and chemistry at his boarding school, had a spark of invention: we needed a lamp for our cubbyhouse, tucked beneath the old stables.

I adored him, his brightness, his confidence. He'd earned a bursary to a GPS school in the city. I followed him like sunlight across water. I carried the jar of methylated spirits slowly, carefully, the glass heavy in my small hands. I didn't yet know "metho" meant danger.

I tripped. The contents drenched my sandshoes and socks, but enough remained to fuel our lamp. The bottle, an old Saxby and Coleman ginger beer bottle, was filled. He fetched a wick, torn from the cord of his pyjama pants, and with a stick poked it into the bottle until a stub protruded. He handed me the matchbox. I lit the wick.

It dropped.

The explosion bloomed at my feet, too hot for him to hold. He ran. And then, I was alight.

Thank God I was a tomboy. If I'd worn a dress, perhaps the fire would have swallowed me whole. Instead, the hand-me-down green boy shorts from Mrs D's garbage bags saved me. Still, my legs burned, and the metho-soaked sandshoes kept feeding the flames.

Nana couldn't hear my screams. I had to run. I was fire, begging for water. She emerged finally, fumbling with a hose, struggling to connect it to the tap, aiming blindly as I kept running.

### Next Foot Forward

In that moment, time warped. I was no longer nine. I was matter, blurred, scattered, and somehow deaf.

My time had become a lost space as I exploded. I was not nine anymore; I was just matter, undefined. By the time the hose sizzled my legs out, my three siblings had long since run away. My brother had to stomp out the fire that had started in our cubbyhouse before he cleared out. My brothers and sister all probably thought they were going to get strapped because we were all involved with matches. They hid across the road inside Mr Snead's shed, which was a forbidden place to us. Brave of them, I reckon.

"She burnt for at least eleven minutes," said the doctor to my parents. I overheard that as I lay face down on the hospital bed. I do not think I had tears on my face, but I had been yelling a lot. I was the brave kid in the town who was always picked to be the first one to get vaccinations when the government people came to our rural towns. We all had to be lined up, either outside the picture theatre or at the showground. "Lina, come and get up the front of the line," said an official when he found me in the crowd. I was always dragged to be first in line. Forgive my lack of memory here, but I really do not know why I was known as the kid who would not cry or flinch. Our town's population at that time was about 12,000, so there must have been other children not scared of needles.

# Chapter 6

My mother was a beautiful and graceful lady who was very keen on appearances. I suspect she was vain, and appearances meant more to her than anything else. "She was dangerously narcissistic, Lina," opined my therapist. Mother worried what people might think, and we heard that phrase often. I sat down and looked at my burnt legs. "Oh! Mother is going to be so angry at this mess," was the first thought in my head. (Twenty years later, I had that very same thought when I was arrested by the police on the island of Okinawa.)

I had to do something quickly or I would be in trouble, so I proceeded to try and brush and scrape off all the black and grey stuff from my legs. I came to bone and remnants of tendon behind my right ankle. How utterly brave I was. Then I remember how very cold and shivery I became.

Fortunately, Mr A, our neighbour, poked his head over the palings and saw the situation. Not really a situation, I suppose, just me on the ground with blackened legs and a Nana wringing her hands at the back steps.

Mr A was a portly, wealthy farmer who could afford to live in town and have a manager working his properties. He wore braces that struggled to stretch over his huge belly.

Back to the burnt legs, though. Mr A was the only person in the street with a car, and he drove it around to the front of our house. I was able to walk to it. He drove to the ambulance station. No one knew quite what to do. They doused my burnt legs with methylated spirits, then loosely wrapped soft gauze around them and told him to take me home. I never understood why no one thought of taking me to the hospital emergency room. Whenever I am mixing up shellac for an artwork, the metho almost knocks me down with its memory smell.

## Next Foot Forward

Mr A drove by my mother's place of business but, as it was her busy time, she told him to take me home and they would deal with it later. My mother had the first women's boutique in the town, and her customers surged to her shop during their lunchtime. In those days, everyone had a full hour for their lunch and could go to the bank, shop, or even visit the dentist.

My mother was also the first clothing shop to give her customers what were called "approval" accounts. This way, they could take the outfit by paying a small percentage, then pay it off each week. They received a little book with the details of their purchase, showing the amount to be repaid. Faithfully, each week they paid and were always buying new things, so my mother was always making money. Lunch break was her busiest time.

"Dealing" with it became changing stinking bandages each evening at the hospital. There was no treatment that fixed full-thickness burns. You just had to hope that they would heal or not. My father, the man with a beautiful tenor voice and strong arms, carried me there each afternoon when he got home from work, because by then the infections had stopped me from walking.

I may need a trigger warning here because there is no avoiding this smelly ugliness.

Treatment involved removing puke-making bandages, laying pieces of crystalline called bluestone, what I now know as copper sulphate, onto the raw and smelly backs of my legs. Bluestone is an odourless and highly toxic compound; it put me in agonising pain which continued for two hundred and forty-three days. Only my doctor could do this, in the hospital's operating theatre, after all the other operations were over for the day.

Going into the theatre after being carried through the dark and gloomy hospital corridors was always a shock. The space was glaringly white and huge, and I lay face down while he slowly unbandaged my legs, from ankles to above my knees. I feel my face wincing as I write this, and I steel myself for the last bit where the bandage stuck tight to the rancid flesh at the back of my ankle. I would look over my shoulder as I lay on that operating table while the final bandages worked loose. The back of my leg looked like a kilo of minced beef shot through with pus and puddles of stinking juice. Even now, I still wake in the night, and the smell of my burnt and rotten flesh is lodged deep inside the mucous membranes of my sinuses.

For the first four months my mother had not come to the hospital, and one night she accompanied us. The doctor told her she could not come into the sterile theatre. However, she was like a force, and eventually he made her put on a gown and cap and let her in. I smile as I write this, and feel a great deal of satisfaction, because as he gradually unwound the bandages and the horrible odour took over the air, my mother fainted just from the smell! The doctor was not the slightest bit sympathetic! My father and I had been enduring that rancid smell for months.

The doctor took no pity on her and nonchalantly kicked a stool under her as she slumped. She never wanted to come to the treatment room with us again. I cannot tell you how much it hurt having that bluestone inside my bandages on my rotten flesh, because even now I can only compare it to childbirth, and it was far worse because it was relentless and stretched ahead to infinity in my child-mind. Worse still was the realisation that I might never be able to run into the surf and roll in the sand on a sunny day. That thought tucked itself somewhere in my brain, behind my ear, and at least once a day it would scurry down into my belly and grip me with fear and desolation. I am the child of the ocean-womb.

Nuns and priests could do no wrong in my parents' eyes. I got caned once in third class because my stool broke. When I told my mother, she replied, "You must have deserved it!" We would have gone without food if the church needed it. The family befriended by the parish curate was considered halfway up to heaven. My parents were determined that we would be that family.

### Next Foot Forward

I, the member of the family thought to be "off with the fairies" or a victim of wild imagination, was the one who loved going off to the six o'clock morning mass. There, especially on Mondays, I found men I believed were "holy" asleep in the church pews at the back. I would gather them up and lead them proudly to my house, bringing them inside and introducing them to my parents. I made their breakfasts, and once I incurred my mother's wrath by dragging one filthy old man into our bathroom and running a bath for him.

I think my parents knew I was trying to be a good Christian, but after I had farewelled the men, I would be told they were just drunks. How can anyone tell a six-year-old child that a human being is just "a drunk"! I remember once convincing my father to give his good shoes to a barefooted man. My father lifted me to the window as the man walked away and said, "Now, Pet. Watch. He'll take those shoes off and sell them for his next bottle of plonk." And that is exactly what happened. He had only gone about ten metres before removing my father's good leather shoes.

Father Denis, our parish's new curate, was Irish and drove into town in a shiny black Holden. We stood out at Sunday mass because we were always scrubbed up and our mother made all our clothes, even our overcoats. On top of that, our father was the soloist, the Italian tenor with a voice to cry about, in the church choir. If you ever heard my father sing *Panis Angelicus* in that beautiful Our Lady of the Rosary church with its high domed ceiling, you, too, would get goosebumps, as I do now just remembering.

One morning, in my bedbound prison and weary of my tortured legs, my heart lifted in relief when I heard the priest's car pull up in front of our house. All day, our house was left unlocked because I was unable to get out of bed. The town's Literary Institute librarian allowed me to borrow as many books as I wished, of any genre, but I grew tired of reading endlessly.

## Adelina Basile

The gate swung open, and I heard footsteps coming up the front path and onto our timber veranda. They were light, leathered footsteps with a bounce to them. When Father Denis's ruddy Irish face and bright blue eyes appeared around the doorway, my sore and tight body relaxed, simply because someone in the world knew I was alive and alone. Oh, to have someone to talk to! To hear a human voice, this one with a rhythmic Irish brogue. To have my long and tangled hair brushed slowly and tenderly as we talked about my schoolwork, the catechism questions for my confirmation, and the doings of the rest of my family.

"What can I do for you, eh Pet? For sure, you must be aching, lying there all day long. Let me ease your back. Here, I brought you a sweetie. Mrs Gleeson is forever baking them for me. Let's get you fattened up, you poor wee thing."

He was my faithful visitor, calling in about five days a week.

I was able to be confirmed ten months later and made my way down the long central aisle of the church on donated children's crutches, padded in cloth the colour of Our Lady blue by the church ladies. I was to have some major operations when I was about sixteen, but the doctor had already saved my right leg and could do no more. Blessed Martin de Porres had given my father his miracle!

Both legs were bandaged, pristine white, from foot to mid-thigh, and I suspect the whole breath-holding congregation was silently hoping I would reach the bishop, waiting benignly before the altar, without falling flat on my face. Today, it would have been the perfect photo opportunity for a bishop!

Next Foot Forward

# Chapter 7

My father was a truly devout man, the son of an Aeolian/Sicilian father and a Venetian mother. He once sent a letter to somewhere in South America asking for a relic of Blessed Martin de Porres. He knew the litany of every saint off by heart and could even tell us how they died. It seems that Blessed Martin (not yet a saint at the time) had captured his imagination because he believed Martin was a doctor. He was not. He was a Dominican lay brother and was later canonised by Pope John XXIII. Looking him up on the internet, I discovered he is the patron saint of "barbers, innkeepers, public health workers, mixed-race people, all those seeking racial harmony, and animals." Oh, my darling Father! Was it my mixed blood that worried you?

The relic arrived in the mail. It was a small rectangular piece of cardboard with a little round window containing a tiny piece of cloth. As soon as we returned from the hospital after my nightly bandaging, I had to press the relic down into my bandages because my father wanted a miracle. The very next evening, the atheist Scottish doctor with the violent temper would undo the smelly rags, find the relic, and toss it onto the floor. Father always rescued it, dusted it off, and whispered as he handed it back to me, "Just have faith, Pet," knowing I would slip it back into my bandages as soon as he carried me home. I learnt early to hope for miracles and to place my faith in Blessed Martin. We did this for ten and a half months, and I am sure I made things worse by sticking my unsterile school ruler down my bandages during the day, poking at the pain to better endure it. At age nine I learnt that if you hurt pain, you gain some relief.

Even though I was young for sixth class, I was eligible to sit an exam that could grant me a scholarship to a Catholic boarding school. Michael, my eldest brother, had won such a bursary two years earlier. My father, who adored and was adored by the nuns, arranged for the exam to come to my house, together with a supervising nun. Sister Bede stood tall in the entrance to the hallway. She was a gentle person, but her face looked as though it had been caught between lift doors as they closed. I thought she resembled a pelican. Her hands, unscarred and beautifully white, clasped the precious exam papers. Murmuring his pleasure at having such a holy woman in the house, Father purred, "Come, Sister. Please, sit."

Plumping me up on heaps of pillows, he ran to the kitchen and returned with the heavy wooden tray, its edges painted with bluebirds. "This will do for her desk. She cannot move her legs or sit in a chair yet."

I was given three pencils that came with the exam. "Can't I use your pen, Father?" He had a beautiful red and gold striped fountain pen I had been using since I first learnt to write. Its nib was gold and so soft on paper. But I had to use pencil. It was a 2B. I loved exams and enjoyed filling white paper with any kind of marks, so I took to my task with gusto.

"If she is successful, we will hold her position. We realise it will be a while before she might be able to leave home," Sister Bede said as she rose in a single movement, brushed her hands of imaginary biscuit crumbs, and handed Father her cup and saucer.

Thinking back, I find it difficult to accept that more than a decade after the end of World War Two, doctors in regional Australia did not know about antibiotics or proper pain relief. When I was alone in that bed, trying to make friends with my agony without antibiotics or painkillers, I grew into one of the most courageous creatures in the world. Like a modern Joan of Arc!

# Chapter 8

I have begun to realise that recalling past events from my troubled life is giving me some insight into my current self. I take a deep breath of this wonderful salty air and cast myself into the sunshine. It is this place that helps me ponder the hurtful parts of my life and is where I receive my consolation.

The sun is a sneaky and sensuous thing, tempting me to dream and then, when my mind has trekked back to that young me in another far-off life, it becomes obvious that I struggled and was caught, not much differently to a fish on a well-sharpened hook.

We lived in a wide street in a town that only stirred with purpose at dawn and again at dusk. In between, it sagged into itself silently and waited. From my bed, I could hear its humid breathing, a slow exhale of stillness punctuated by the occasional birdcall or the rustling of trees that guarded our gate like reluctant sentries.

The house I lived in was large and wooden, typical of early Australian country homes. Lofty ceilings loomed above me like a chapel, and inside there were no doors—only yawning passageways that gave the house its own language. Floorboards creaked and settled, speaking in sighs and groans that I came to understand more intimately than human voices. I imagined the walls listened back, remembering families that once filled their corners with laughter and footsteps. I became fluent in the dialect of emptiness without even knowing.

There was no one home. From eight o'clock each morning, the others—my family—were swallowed by school or work. I remained, a girl alone in a house that didn't close behind them. The side verandah and the front gate watched me from afar, half-forgotten sentinels. No one locked the doors. There was no need. Not for me.

## Adelina Basile

My legs had gone gangrenous. The doctors used phrases like *full thickness burns*, whispered near my bed in tones they thought I couldn't hear and words they assumed I wouldn't understand. *Amputation* was a word they passed between themselves in sterile corridors, as if it belonged to someone else. I couldn't walk. Could barely shift the heavy limbs attached to me, they had become foreign, burdensome things I had to lift with my hands just to turn on my side. I was no longer part of the world that moved, even within my own skin.

I could tell the time by the chorus outside, the shuffle of school shoes, the rumble of engines, the fading conversations of postmen and housewives. After the morning rush faded into silence, the house would settle again. I too tried to settle, pretending not to exist. Pretending invisibility was a kind of choice.

This was when I began to build the world inside, a private place that wasn't broken, wasn't overlooked. In my imagination, the girl in bed had agency, purpose, and I strove for my own power. I trained my thoughts like stretched elastic across the windows of this new inner world, wrapping them around truth and pain, making something stronger than both. I could not yet identify what I was trying to overcome. Outside, the world had no need for me. I wasn't even a comma in its grand design. But inside, I was the architect.

I wonder now if anyone ever thought I might feel alone. Not just on that day, but every day since. The loneliness wasn't loud. It was soft, insistent, and daily. Kids skipped past my windows, shouting about spelling tests or lunch money. Cars took people to their workplaces. I lay still and listened, like a forgotten note in a symphony that didn't miss its absence. Like the broken string on my mother's mandolin that she somehow managed to avoid as she played *Beautiful Dreamer* in the night after dinnertime. The house would settle into silence again, and I would learn, without bitterness, that significance was not something given to us at birth, it was something I'd need to carve myself.

## Next Foot Forward

Excruciating pain became just "four letters." I quickly taught myself to change them inside my head... *d o g s, p l u m*... and so on until *p a i n* meant nothing. It's like that with children who are all alone and trying to make sense of a situation. We become innovative. What else could a child do?

The Basile family, my family, being Irish-Italian, was Catholic to its core. Weekly Mass, Friday Stations of the Cross, daily family rosary, prayer cards for birthdays, and all the other nonsense. I was a Child of Mary every second Sunday; my sister was a Child of Ann on the alternate one. My cloak was blue and hers was red. Both my brothers were altar boys, and my father was the best tenor in town, celebrated for his voice.

In the middle of winter, our family bundled up and made our way to the church for benediction. The night was cold and crisp, the air biting at our cheeks as we hurried inside. I had discovered a nest of tiny field mice earlier that day and, as the animal rescuer in the family, decided to bring them along, tucked safely in the pocket of my overcoat.

The church was warm and filled with the soft glow of candlelight, casting flickering shadows on the walls and making interesting shapes on the Stations of the Cross, which were carved in relief, in marble. The congregation gathered, everyone nodding and greeting each other until the organ struck the first chords of *O Salutaris Hostia*. The service began. I knelt with my family, head bowed, feeling the comforting weight of the mice in my pocket.

As the benediction reached its most sacred part, when the priest held the shining golden monstrance up to bless us, a sudden commotion broke the solemn silence. The mice, perhaps sensing the warmth and light, wriggled free from my pocket and scattered across the floor. Confusion rippled through the congregation as people gasped and murmured, peering left and right while trying to understand the source of the disturbance.

Peace was shattered, replaced by a flurry of movement and whispered exclamations. I remained kneeling, head bowed, heart pounding with a mix of guilt and excitement. It didn't take long for everyone to realise the culprit. I was the only one still in prayerful posture. My posture must have been screaming *guilty*.

**Next Foot Forward**

# Chapter 9

Here I am, greying at the temples yet still feeling that sense of preciousness that Father Denis bestowed on me at nine years of age. I was trapped as a hummingbird gets, in a huntsman spiderweb by that priest, and I hovered for the next four and a half years, sipping the nectar of goodness and the Holy Spirit.

For the next four years, Father Denis used to pick me for all kinds of jobs and favours, and I think he was one of the reasons I made no friends. His favourite thing was to pick me up and sit me in the front seat beside him. It was a bench seat. Seatbelts didn't exist. He liked me to lie my head in his lap and would drive while stroking my head. I felt bewildered, but cared for, and did not have a brain to wonder why. Besides, being stroked or petted was not something that happened in my family. Father Denis had a peculiar odour that I could not identify until I was married. It was the smell of stale semen.

The other reason I was friendless was the fact that I was not allowed to play sport or ride a bike because the skin on my legs was prone to ulceration, and I was still too small to have any large-scale skin grafts. The only freedom that my body really experienced was when I was taken to our beach, where my legs were covered in Vaseline and Ungivita cream while I was in the surf. There, I felt as light as an angel as my skin soothed itself in the churning agitation of a cheeky wave.

I was a great reader, as I have mentioned, and to this day remember a book called *Andersonville*, because I could relate to horribly injured soldiers very well. The author was MacKinlay Kantor, and it told of a terrible Confederate prisoner-of-war camp and gave me nightmares. I also had nightmares after seeing pictures of Auschwitz, Bergen-Belsen, and all the other inhuman acts of which humankind is capable. As I write, there are people being swept up in the United States and just disappeared for no reason other than they are the wrong colour or trying to find a better life.

## Adelina Basile

Some of them are just sent to foreign prisons without recourse to any representation for justice.

I do remember buying my first ever fiction: Alexandre Dumas' *The Black Tulip*. I was so proud of it, but when my father looked inside the cover and found it did not have the approval of the Church, an *imprimatur*, he burnt it. It is hard to have a book burnt when you are twelve, and I cannot imagine how countries can burn or ban any books, anywhere.

When I was thirteen, I had been the priest's favourite for about four years. I went with my church group and Father Denis on a hike into wilderness outside our town. Five of us squashed into his car, excited to explore. This was serious, uncharted, and rugged mountainous country. We left the car at the school in Upper Lansdowne and, without any experience or emergency equipment, started crawling and stretching ourselves up a steep mountainside. This was logging country, but even the mobile sawmills did not venture to set up work on this steep mountain ridge.

Ridges were so steep that when I looked down, every bit of land fell away far below my toes. Crossing a creek, the priest stumbled in the freezing water and lost our only compass. Our packed lunches were eaten as we found a relatively level hillock, and as the sun was still out, we felt confident that we would soon find our way out. After about seven hours of struggling through thick underbrush beneath giant gum trees packed close together, and climbing dangerously rocky parapets in the hope of finding a landmark, we all knew we were lost. Light was stolen from us swiftly, and a gloom descended on us all. No one spoke any more. We were three girls and two boys, the latter so scared we had to push them up the steep mountainside. This was thick, wild, and untouched state forest. My chafed thighs trembled from exertion, and shivers overtook the rest of my body. Night fell.

"Gather up some bark from over there," pointed Father Denis, his face dark and saturnine, not the usual rosy, smiling face dear to

## Next Foot Forward

me. "Find yourselves a place and cover up. We'll say a decade of the Glorious Mysteries." He indicated one of the boys, John, to start. We mumbled beneath our bark until all was quiet, except for the skittering beneath the forest floor from creatures I had to imagine. Maybe a spotted quoll, voracious and carnivorous in its russet coat, might slink out from the understorey to investigate human intruders. I had longed to see one since I read the museum's *Book of Australian Mammals*.

Earlier, I had picked some purple and juicy lilly-pillies while we were wandering, as I had read that they were edible as a native food, and I had observed birds eating them while we trekked. While I chewed, all the juices dried in my mouth as if my mucous skin had shrunk, and I spat it out.

Dingoes were howling to our west and then from all around us, as if we were inside their bowl. Their vocabulary was complex as they chattered, growled, snorted, howled, and sometimes even purred. Eerily, they reminded me of calves lost and calling to their mothers, which had been loaded into cattle trucks and off to saleyards. We could hear gunshots, so we knew that the police were looking for us, but they were far away, and it was cold. Earlier, the thunk, thunk, thunk of a helicopter had cheered us up, but as the evening darkened and the forest thickened, the chopper faded away.

I had gone on this hike with my second-ever period. These were the days of no tampons; feminine hygiene products were still a thing of the future, and my mother seemed incapable of explaining menstruation to me. There had been no opportunity to change the pad even if my mother had given me one, and as the day got longer, I became increasingly uncomfortable. I could smell myself and had chafed thighs. Embarrassed by my odour, I moved away from the others and lay under a layer of grey gum bark close to the deep forest edge.

## Adelina Basile

During that night, I was woken by Father Denis' hand over my mouth. His other hand was deep inside my virginal, bloody vagina as though he were searching for something. I turned into a stone, and he touched and squeezed, totally violating me. His hands slid up under my jumper and grabbed my breast flesh as if he were gripping a steering wheel. It hurt. It smelt. It put me to despair. I think I was too stunned or shocked to call out, and that sullying act has followed me my entire life. That loss of voice belies the profound issue in which one feels compromised. In my case, it stalled my sense of identity and self-expression. I was known in our family as being "away with the fairies," even though no one knew of this violation for at least forty years. The hummingbird was violently dispatched by the raptor.

Our hiking group was found late the next afternoon by one of the many search parties. We were driven into town on the back of a timber lorry. We were news by then, so the entire town was clustered along the main streets, cheering and waving. The parents of my friends were waiting outside the post office, but no one from my family was there.

When I finally arrived home, it was as if the trauma had spilled outward and leaked into the yard. My father was in the back garden, vomiting so violently he'd nearly desiccated. For two days, he'd been unravelling in parallel. I have mentioned his nervous disposition before. My mother, responding in the only way she knew, had baked herself numb. Every surface—table, bench, windowsill—was buried under sponges and biscuits, as if sweetness might drown the horror.

I collapsed into bed, bloodied and smelling of forest, of violation, of fear. For three days, I slept—deep and dark, dreamless.

And when I woke... there were words in my head, countless, crowding. But my tongue, my lips, my mouth had become mutinous. I was mute.

## Next Foot Forward

Not from injury. Not from physical damage. But from something deeper: looking back, and with the help of my therapist, I realise my muteness was the result of the extinguishing of trust, the erasure of safe expression. I had been silenced not just by Father McAlinden, but by the world of mine, which could not bear the weight of my truth. No one knew why I suddenly stopped speaking. I was labelled dreamy, fairy-struck, lost in the clouds. And maybe I was.

Because my words had taken flight like that hummingbird—fragile, brilliant, impossible to grasp. And the raptor had come.

The first psychiatrist I was sent to was in a big city to the south of our town. He was young, redheaded, and informed me that he was recently married. He told jolly tales of his life as a newly married man but was unable to loosen my words, which were stuck deep beneath my heart and tongue. Today, while I remember my memories, at that time all I really needed was an arm around me and permission to have a broken heart.

"Has she had a shock of any kind?" asked the doctor. "Physically, she is fit as a fiddle."

Both parents shook their heads, quite bewildered and unable to think what might have caused me to lose my words. I remember now that after my burns had healed enough for me to be mobile, the doctor had told Mother that "the shock of such burns has to come out of your daughter, now or later." I think my mother had not grasped that notion.

Losing trust when you are a child has significant impact on your life. For various reasons, I could not trust the church, my parents, or my siblings. I held love for them, but I suspect I somehow withdrew and chose solitude because I have no happy memories from then. From birth, I had been considered by the family to be "a bit different" and "prone to imagination" or "off with the fairies." My sleepwalking became a nuisance for my parents, and

## Adelina Basile

I had an ability to take myself out of my body and watch my world from afar.

Reader, I know now that shock sent me mute, but the thought of telling my parents what Father Denis did to me never crossed my mind. If I were going to tell on a priest, I thought that my father's heart would break! My parents would be so hurt, or worse still, they would have thought that I had imagined things. They loved him as a family friend. One who, for a whole year, had kept me company as I lay alone with my burnt legs. Imagine how angry my mother would be at me. No. In my mind, I already had a strong steel storage box. My life was too weird to be shared, and I was too frightened of hurting people or making them feel guilty. The five years of being petted and mauled, fingered, and poked, including the long car trips for whole weekends, all got edited into one single file and put in that steel box next to the "burnt leg," "mafia," and "body bags" files. That file was called "Fr McAlinden."

The second doctor was also a psychiatrist. By then I could answer basic questions that required a one-word response but could not initiate a conversation. After three visits, the doctor informed my parents that this was the delayed shock resulting from my massive burn experience, and it was natural that it had happened. He called it a nervous breakdown and suggested that a few weeks at the beach would be restorative for me. My current therapist discovered that I disassociated—and I still do. The memories I am writing about are my only ones. I wish I could remember all the things my brothers talk about, but they are somewhere inside that big, locked file in my brain.

Remembering that passage of my childhood has me rushing us to my scrubby dunes. I am shaking with caffeine and need the sea air on my skin. Wedged between these dunes and the sea live four scrubby hills that feed our wetlands. Although I can still watch the bird-swirling headland and smell the rotting seagrass on the shore, I meet me, whole and full, without prejudice. It is strangely painful

### Next Foot Forward

being completely present. I need a zipper down my back to loosen my skin. Antoine de Saint-Exupéry said that "Life always bursts the boundaries of formulas," and I realise that I am making my own formulas, for the first time.

Sitting here, safe and sure, I write a poem to myself, like a growth line on a bone:

## Adelina Basile

**Last Summer**

*The summer's over now, the southerly is strong, I stroll along the beach*

*No rubbish to step on, the dunes are stronger too*

*Without the trash and silt, and tides have caught the ruins*

*Of castles I once built. Waves are breaking cleanly*

*Onto firm brown sand. A lone boardrider silhouetted,*

*Marching to his band. Somehow blending into nature*

*Bliss etched on his face, easily blending into nature*

*Rejoicing in his space.*

*The winter birds are back, swooping low and gay,*

*Catching sight of glitter fish darting through the spray,*

*Not screaming like the gulls or eagles of great might,*

*Just little birds flying for fun and sheer delight.*

*Remember that young gull? I spoke to him in French*

*And fed him on salami scraps. He balanced on the bench.*

*I made him feel superior that far-off summer day.*

*I wonder—did he visit back when I had gone away?*

*I ponder where he is. Will instinct bring him back*

*When the sun is strong and the east wind blows*

*And humans make their tracks*

*Upon this silent sweep of shore, that's purely mine today.*

**Next Foot Forward**

*Last Summer—gold and gentle time. But still, my yesterday.*

# Chapter 10

Boarding school, an all-girls academic one, seemed the best option for me once my voice returned, and I still had the scholarship I'd won back in sixth grade. It was arranged that a nun would come and massage my legs in the mornings, before early Mass, so I could walk. That was my most painful and challenging time. I still had ligament damage and muscle atrophy, and after almost a year of being bedridden, no one had thought to organise any rehabilitation. My legs needed more surgery, but that couldn't be done until I was close to full growth.

The calm quietude suited my nature, as did the regimentation of each day. Every minute was accounted for, and life for me became study, lessons, and sleep. I developed a hatred of sago pudding but a love for the smell of lemon wax and freshly baked bread. Tuesdays were wonderful, as we were obliged to converse in French, and on Sundays, I think the chef nun had the day off. Our dinner was fresh bread, butter, and honey. My mouth still fills with saliva even now as I recall that long-ago Sunday meal.

We weren't permitted to go home during the twelve-week terms but were allowed a family visit once a month. My parents would drive down for a Sunday afternoon, bringing rhubarb and folios of paper that the nuns adored receiving from my father. I can't remember what we did in the idle hours before they drove off again.

The school motto was *Strength in Difficulties*, a motto I could proudly identify with, and the school was renowned for gaining Commonwealth and Teachers' scholarships.

I was as smart as a whip but terrified at the thought of entering such a large, strange building. I didn't know then that I was autistic, but changes like this were truly terrifying, as I could never read the signals people's bodies gave or understand the meanings behind what they said. Mother and Father drove me there the first time, and we were interviewed in a high-ceilinged room that smelled of lemons and wax. The nuns belonged to the Order of the Black St Josephs, famous now because of their founder, Saint Mary MacKillop.

Having spent almost a year flat on my back with nothing to do but read, I had devoured every book on art and famous artists. I pleaded to be allowed to take Art as a major subject. However, Sister Stephanie, the senior education nun, explained to my parents that she wasn't happy with the quality or outcomes of the Art teacher. She told them earnestly, "We hold a prestigious reputation for our final results and win scholarships each year. I'm not sure that Art would help us maintain that reputation. Lina would do well with Biology as a science. We have an excellent teacher."

Probably, Sister Stephanie was the only woman in the world who could challenge my mother.

The nun carried my suitcase, a small, battered thing with a stubborn clasp, and led me up the stairs. My legs, still burnt and bandaged, had already been entrusted to nurses and strangers. My parents had gone.

The junior dormitory opened before me like a hangar of silence. Rows of metal beds stretched deep into the room, too many to count, like grave markers in some antiseptic field. Each had a thin mattress and a grey blanket, folded with military precision. Beside them stood the "wardrobes": tiny metal tables with nothing to hide behind.

Everything was in straight lines. No colour. No sound. No warmth.

I didn't know where I was meant to sleep. I didn't know anyone's name.

And I still don't. My mind has always been generous in its forgetting. Over the years, it has blurred the faces and erased the voices, a kindness born from trauma. *Dissociative amnesia*, they call it. But I mourn the memory just the same. That dormitory remains like a dream half-remembered, a place made of angles and shame.

I was clever. Not because anyone taught me to be, but because I lived in books. I had no peer group, no friends, no one to mirror or muffle my thoughts. I didn't know I was autistic then, only that I listened more than I spoke and heard the edges of things most others missed.

School was a place I navigated by instinct, by listening, not just with my ears but with every atom of attention.

After dinner, there was a gift I cherished: study hall. A room of quiet minds and page turns. The scent of floor polish lingered beneath thin socks and restless wooden chairs. Every sound was intimate, papers rustling, pencils tapping, bodies wriggling against discipline. It soothed me. I was finally among other minds, not bodies.

The nuns who taught me, I realise now, were brilliant women cloaked in habits and mystery. They didn't know they were shaping a sanctuary for me. Sister Joseph, tall and stark against the pale window light, spoke of empires, elephants, and philosophy as if she'd lived among them. She barely moved, just stood with one hand curled under the other, eyes like misted glass, speaking entire worlds into existence. She was my Ancient History teacher. As she spoke, I was far away in time, riding on the back of one of Hannibal's elephants as we crossed the mountains. But truly, she was a time-traveller, and I, seated in the third row, was always ready to follow.

At the end of my final year, I had secured the promise of a scholarship, and my heart was heavy as I made my final goodbyes to boarding school.

## Next Foot Forward

Before I could continue with my life, I needed more plastic surgery. I had completed high school at sixteen and was set to commence a scholarship in the June intake. However, I had grown sufficiently for the specialist doctor in Sydney to undertake the major skin grafts my legs required. Until then, I had been unable to engage in activities that might impact the backs of my legs, preventing me from riding bikes or playing sport. The surgery was performed, and I was hospitalised for about five weeks, my right leg encased in a thick plaster bandage.

I was placed in Gloucester House, a part of the hospital where my ward resembled a vast hall filled with beds. For some reason, I felt as though I was in a Charles Dickens story. Hospital beds always seem lonely to me, even when they're occupied. My bed was situated towards the back, about four beds in from a window. Green-grey lino covered the floor of that vast auditorium, and our beds were lined up in such perfect rows you'd swear they'd been drawn on paper with a set square.

Early each morning, a squad of moppers would arrive, one platoon with wet mops and buckets, followed by a second platoon to dry and smooth until the lino sparkled again.

By this stage of my life, I had become accustomed to pain and to the futility of acknowledging it. The pain was immense. Each morning, the doctor, standing tall in his suit with a vest and a stripey tie, his hands clasped behind his back, would stop by my bed with raised eyebrows. Beside him stood his nursing sister, crackling starchily in white and wearing a veil with four navy stripes. She would smile at me and inquire about my condition.

"How are you today, dear?"

I responded as I had been taught, "Very well, thank you."

She barely reached the doctor's shoulder but would half-bow to me, turn her head to him, and gesture towards the next patient on their list.

## Adelina Basile

One day, after I had been in hospital for about eight days, my mother travelled from the country to visit me and found me asleep, tears staining my face. She confronted the doctor, demanding to know why I was crying. Perhaps I was crying because I was once again alone, a long way from home and the beach. My days were unbearably long in that place. There were no visitors.

When they removed the plaster, which extended from my toe to above my knee, they discovered a severe infection and an allergic reaction to the dressing. It was such a traumatic experience that I refused to have my other leg repaired.

When I won the scholarship to Teachers' College, I moved into a boarding house in the city, unaware of the social life that buzzed beneath the surface. I approached college with the same discipline and structure I'd carried through school. It was a pleasure mastering assignments and studying diligently. I worked as if I were still in uniform.

But I didn't know there were places to meet people, spaces meant for laughter and belonging. That absence defined me. While others formed friendships and networks, I existed just outside the edges. To this day, I can recall the names of only two girls and three nuns, despite three full years of shared rooms, meals, and routines.

Fifteen years of intensive education had passed, yet I had never made a best friend. Never found my way into a group. I was bright, exceptionally so, but my brightness existed alone. I didn't yet know I was autistic. I just knew I listened more than I spoke, studied while others socialised, and carried my knowledge like a shield.

This isolation was formative. I didn't just miss out on friendship; I missed out on learning how to be part of something. That loss, over so many years, left more than silence. It left spaces that trauma filled.

## Next Foot Forward

Looking out at my beach and village now, I'm grateful that although it's far more populated and termed the *"Pearl of the Coast"* by our council, its basic geography has kept it from being overdeveloped. Behind the hill to the south, the land belongs to the National Parks and Wildlife Service and will not be developed. It's a haven for swamp wallabies. I've become quite expert in the care and rehabilitation of this species, and they are dear to my soul. These fascinating marsupials have one fewer chromosome than all other species of macropod. Most others live in mobs and are grass or pasture eaters, which makes them pests to our graziers.

Swamp wallabies, with their dark charcoal coats, have chosen solitude. There are no mobs or groups. Herbs and native grasses make up their diet, and as a result, they have a scent that wrinkles people's noses. I love it, it's deeply eucalypt, with overtones of leaf matter. Each morning, as I stride along the track while the dew still shines, there's one I call *my friend*. He stands like a chunky stump, small arms held close to his chest, eyes following my every movement. We nod a greeting, and he lowers his head back to nibble at the native rosemary. I relate to their need for solitude and their silent, intense observation of life.

A few years ago, I rescued a female with a joey the size of a peanut in her pouch. She was the victim of a car accident, her left arm so severely injured that she couldn't have survived. My veterinarian, well accustomed to me by then after years of wildlife rescues, offered to perform extremely delicate surgery and ordered a prosthesis that had to be imported from Germany. I agreed to the cost of six hundred dollars, and the vet gave his time for free.

By then I had named her Jessie, and over the next four months, I had the joy of watching her and her joey, Bessie, as they grew and recovered. Jessie was successfully released on a nearby farm. A few months later, as I wandered through the bush, I heard a soft, padding thump on the leaf litter. There she was, unafraid and calm enough to recline near me, loosening the purse strings of her pouch to show off her baby. Encounters like this are exceptionally rare, as once we "wild" our native creatures, we rarely know their outcomes.

During my early years, this small beachside village was little more than a hamlet surrounded by dairy farms. It was a safe beach, curved to face the south. A row of Norfolk pines bordered the village edge onto the sand, and the rest of the dunes were fenced off. I always thought it was to stop the cows from wandering into the ocean and drowning.

No one taught us to swim when we were kids. We all learned to bodysurf first, then later developed our own strokes. We had a shark tower, although I only ever saw one lifesaver sitting up there. He perched with his back against one of the giant tripod logs, cigarette smoke curling up from behind the open pages of his broadsheet newspaper.

We were never afraid of the grey nurse sharks that shared the sea with us, sharks that today have just been saved from extinction. We helped the fishermen drag their heavy boats up or down the beach and were rewarded with a lobster or snapper or, my favourite, sea mullet. Neither of my parents could swim. My father was a typical Italian gentleman who couldn't endure water on his head, while my mother wore beautiful swimsuits on her svelte body, smart leather sandals on her narrow feet, and stayed perfectly dry.

A pattern of my early life was one of surfing and fishing, and when the harsh wind riled up the waves, there was always a hollow in the dunes where one could lie and dream or read. On windy afternoons, my brother and I would head into the bush and raid the ring-tailed possum nests. Inside the dune bush, the air was thick with a rancid smell that excited me. The crashing of the waves was muted in that place. The floor was thick with fallen leaves, damp from time and salt, so our excursions were made in silence.

We shook the trees until the baby would fall out of the nest, then tucked it up our sloppy joe sweaters and took them back to our

## Next Foot Forward

shack, where they always escaped into the rafters and roof. Our parents didn't really mind the possums, but we were made to go and stand up to our noses in the surf to kill the ticks. It didn't matter what the weather was, we had to stay underwater until, upon inspection, all the ticks had drowned or dropped off.

Autumns here at Black Head are particularly lovely, the colours, the sounds, the scents. One of those seasons Keats would have written about, I'm sure. Or Browning: *"The grey sea and the long black land, And the yellow half-moon large and low..."* Looking through the lens of the unwavering support of the sky, sand, magpies, waves, and towering trees, I am comfortably safe as I rummage through the past years that were my unruly decades.

Fishing on the beach when you're the sole human is a wondrous thing, an activity I deeply enjoy. I feel that fishing is an ethical sport, especially since tagging and catch-and-release have been encouraged.

Yesterday was one pearler of a day. The air was sweet and clear, quaveringly delicate with a discernible tension of its own. The onshore winds of yesterday had glassed the ocean with two deep, inviting channels, just calling for me and my fishing gear. I grabbed my bucket and rod, took my dog off the lead, and set off.

Here I am, standing on an arc of sand that's marked on maps of *"Coastal Exploration, 1789"*, *Government Gazette*. I found this reference in my father's book on the first exploration of the east coast of Australia.

Using pipi bait, I cast out to the back of the gutter and stayed there for hours, the sun beating on my back, seagull acolytes tripping around my feet or whirling off into the bush when the big Brahminy kite came soaring and circling overhead. Its breast feathers were white as reflected light, contrasting with the beautiful russet bronze of its wings.

## Adelina Basile

I continued to play at fishing as I absorbed the colours, the barrel-shaped clouds and the long blue curve of beach pointing north.

And the sounds! The eternal *shroooom* of small breaking waves, lorikeets in flocks arguing in their feisty, shrill voices, and sand squeaking beneath my feet. Just today, I signed an online petition protesting offshore gas mining, and it's so sad to think that humankind feels the need to impinge upon what is naturally beautiful just to exist.

The beach I'm looking at right now is the place where I borrowed my brother's speargun during one of our long school holidays. I was finally walking again after those long months of solitude and was excited to be back on my beach. I had just started walking and swimming again after all those months in bed.

Michael's speargun was called a *"double-rubber bazooka,"* which I thought was a fantastic name. I decided to have a practice shot.

I'd owned my own little single-shot .22 rifle and had hunted rabbit and fox on a farm a few miles away since I was seven. I was a good shot and familiar with handling weapons. The speargun had been cocked, my brother had stretched the rubbers into firing position, and the stock was made of Australian hardwood. I didn't know that they were meant to be fired only underwater and held at arm's length. So, I tucked it under my chin as best I could and pulled the trigger.

The recoil knocked me flat on my back, killed my front tooth, and split my lip right down to the bottom of my chin. None of my brother's friends could look at me, blood was everywhere. How squeamish are youths who then go to war and kill! One boy asked if I had lost any teeth. I put my tongue to feel, and it went straight through the bottom of my lip. I thought that was my gum, so I told him I'd lost all my lower teeth.

I remember I was wearing those bubble swimmers of the 'fifties, and wet sand filled most of the bubbles.

### Next Foot Forward

It was another trip to an emergency doctor, and I had a six-stitch lip for a month or so. I could look down and see inside my own lip, which makes me smile. Even now, my tongue traces the thick scar on the inside of my lip.

Adelina Basile

# Chapter 11

Reader, are you beginning to see a pattern of life unfolding? Trust me, it gets even more bizarre.

In the early 1960s, I was living in Sydney with my two brothers. We rented a second-storey flat in Railway Street, Petersham, close to the Parramatta Road end. There were four of us, my brothers, one of their friends from home, and myself. We were all students at various colleges or universities. It was then that the events occurred that led to me being kidnapped by three mafia thugs two years later.

In the pale light of a Sydney morning in 1962, I found myself seated in my brother's souped-up Cooper "S" Mini, its engine growling and rumbling in peak hour as we trundled down the familiar streets near Newtown. We were just two second-generation Italians navigating our way through a city that held both promise and prejudice. But while we shared blood and heritage, our hearts were tuned to different frequencies. My brother, hardened by the quiet cruelty of his boarding school years, I think, had absorbed a bitterness that shaped how he saw the world. Racism ran deep in him, casual and vicious, like a language he spoke fluently and without shame.

I, on the other hand, had always found beauty in difference. I loved being dark, being called "liquorice legs" or "dago." It gave me agency somehow. Accents, gestures, skin tones, the tapestry of humanity fascinated me. I was drawn to it, protective of it, perhaps as a way of resisting the narrowness I saw in my own home. The colours and nuances of people were just a part of the nature that I loved.

That morning, our Mini collided with another car, one of those ordinary accidents that spins into something else entirely. The other driver was Sicilian, dark-eyed and angry, his frustration matching my brother's in volume and venom. Their argument

## Next Foot Forward

swelled on the footpath like a storm cloud, shouting, gesturing, their words tangled in rage and history. I stepped in, dragging my brother away as if peeling wax off a surfboard on a hot day. He was drenched with heated anger.

The next day, as sunlight spilled across Parramatta Road, I spotted the same young man, whose name was Giovanni, at the local greengrocer. He approached shyly, speaking broken English, his gratitude clear despite the gaps in grammar. I replied in Italian, relieved and thrilled to finally put my rusty phrases to use. That small exchange opened a doorway to a world I hadn't quite known I was searching for.

Before long, I was embraced by the Italian community in Leichhardt. I loved the mosaic of voices, laughter, and shared meals. They made room for me, not just in their gatherings but in their hearts. It was in their company that I learned a deeper kind of belonging, one rooted not in ancestry alone, but in kindness, curiosity, and the courage to stand apart from hate.

One Sunday, I was lying on Bondi Beach after a surf when Giovanni approached me across the sand, accompanied by two other men. They were all dressed in suits and leather shoes and looked out of place. Without warning, one of the men grabbed my arm and pressed a knife under my armpit. I was told I had to go with them to tell a solicitor that, on a certain night, I had been with Giovanni the entire night. I was seventeen and had never been with another boy, not even on a date! We walked across the sand, and I was put in a car and taken to a building where we all went upstairs, the knife now in my back. So yes, I told the lie.

I shared the house with my two brothers, as we were all country kids. I was alone most of the time after classes, as my brothers always went to the pub after their work or studies, and I had no social life or group of friends. I studied instead.

For the next few months, until I graduated, I was followed everywhere. I don't know how. I would be accosted by Giovanni or another nameless man as I was going in my front door every single afternoon and questioned about everyone I spoke to. How did they know when I used a public phone at a train station?

If they were not satisfied with my answers, they punched me in the face. They threatened to kill both my brothers if I told anyone. I felt very trapped and horribly scared. I made one valiant effort to escape.

Our flat was on the second floor, and I climbed out my bedroom window and slid down the drainpipe. I was hoping to get to a public phone without them seeing me because someone was always on watch at the front road. I had forgotten that there was a very narrow lane, possibly for utilities, as I think back now. As I ran for the side street, they must have seen me.

They caught me, beat me unconscious, and I woke up on the dewy lawn of a doctor's house. I still carry the scar on my lip, and my earlobe had been torn, my favourite pretend emerald earring was gone. The doctor asked no questions; he simply stitched me up. I told my brothers I had tripped down the stairs that led to our flat on the first floor. I didn't try again.

Looking back, I realise I've always had an affinity with the underdog, the misunderstood, and especially with migrants. Perhaps my instinctive defence of Giovanni that day, standing up against my brother's rage, had put me under a spotlight in the Italian community of Leichhardt, where we lived.

When it came time for my block of practice teaching, I chose a primary school far from the city. I thought I'd be safe that far away from the Mafia. It was a little three-teacher school called Gilgai, on the Northern Tablelands near Inverell. It would have been about a ten-hour drive from Sydney, and difficult to reach from my hometown, as there was no direct public transport. Once, my father even hired a small plane to fly me across the range.

## Next Foot Forward

I adored my little schoolhouse. It stood like something out of a fairytale, carved into the hillside and surrounded by camphor laurel trees that shaded the playground like sentinels. My classroom had wide verandahs that caught the breeze when it blew, and inside, thirty-eight children from three different grades filled the space with laughter and trust. We spoke the same language, unspoken, intuitive. Teaching never felt like work; it was as natural as breathing.

I lodged in half of a weatherboard house, connected by a narrow door to the owner, a gentle woman named Mrs Farrand. Life was peaceful, until it wasn't.

I had been subpoenaed to appear in a Sydney courtroom to give false evidence. False. Under oath. The words alone made my chest tighten. I knew I couldn't do it, I wouldn't.

Then came the reckoning.

One afternoon, as the final bell echoed across the school grounds, three men arrived in a dark car. They didn't speak. They positioned themselves on the verandah of my freestanding classroom, silent watchers. My heart crawled into my throat. When the other teacher drove me home, they followed, their headlights like eyes that refused to blink.

"We've come to escort you to Sydney," one said.

I nodded, but inside I was burning with panic. I waited until they were settled in the car outside. Then I slipped through the inner door of my lodgings and begged Mrs Farrand to call the police. She did.

A detective arrived quickly, before I'd even found my toothbrush and a spare pair of undies, I thought I might need. He confronted the men, threw them out of town, and then took me to the station. There, under the harsh fluorescent lights, I finally unravelled everything. I told the detectives everything in order, from my

## Adelina Basile

brother's accident with Giovanni to the moment I was threatened at Bondi Beach, a knife pressed beneath my arm like an omen.

"I can't lie," I told them. "I'm terrified."

That night unfolded like a fever dream. I was placed on a plane under police escort and flown to Sydney under cover of darkness. Somewhere in a tall building, I met a man, perhaps a judge, who dismissed the subpoena as casually as if he were brushing ash from his sleeve. His eyes were tired and bagged, but his smile was gentle, almost reassuring, a silent message of *business as usual*.

"You'll make your statement in Leichhardt, under protection," he said.

And I did. Alone, trembling, I wrote the truth where others had tried to sow lies.

By dawn, I was airborne again, returned to my classroom, to the camphor laurels. But I was not the same.

At the trial, Giovanni was sentenced. As he was led from the courtroom, he turned and screamed through the bars, "I will kill her when I get out!"

Later, we learned he was a lieutenant in the Mafia, wanted for murder in Taormina. My parents were furious that I had become entangled in such a mess. They didn't understand. I told them that without intervention, my brothers might have been killed.

What they couldn't see was the year of silence that followed, a year haunted by shadows in rear-view mirrors and slow footsteps at night. A year stitched with fear, and the slow unravelling of my trust in the world.

**Next Foot Forward**

# Chapter 12

In 1963, I had another nervous breakdown. I was boarding at Kingsford in a house my mother had found through an advertisement in the *Catholic Weekly*. My brothers had gone their own ways, one became a surveyor, the other was training to be a hotel manager, so we'd given up the flat we'd once shared in Petersham.

I was a conscientious student who owned only a few clothes, along with my books and assignments. One of my brother's friends from our hometown, Wayne, was studying economics at Sydney University. Our parents were social friends, and I suspect my mother had asked him to keep an eye on me in the city. When he needed a partner for the university ball at the Roundhouse, I was pleased to be invited, I had no friends in Sydney, so it felt nice to be included by someone familiar.

When we got back to my place around midnight, the woman who owned the house became furious when I tried to make my friend a cup of tea. It had started raining, and I thought a cup of tea might slow Wayne down, as he was a heavy drinker. I had never drunk alcohol, I would always take a thermos of milk if I went somewhere drinks were served. But my landlady gathered up all my clothes, shoes, books, and half-finished assignments and threw them onto the street while screaming at me. Wayne drove off, in shock, I suppose, and when I went outside to collect my belongings, she locked me out of the house.

From that moment until four days later, I have total amnesia. The next thing I remember was four days later, sitting in the rehearsal rooms of Her Majesty's Theatre in Melbourne. Apparently, I had auditioned and gained a part in a production, though I have no idea what role it was. A policewoman entered through a side door and approached me.

"Are you Lina Basile?" she asked.

## Adelina Basile

"Yes," I replied with a smile. "That's who I am."

She told me my father and brother were waiting outside. I followed her out, got into our family car, and we drove the many hours back to my hometown. I don't think any of us said a word.

I spent about three months at home, seeing doctors. I wasn't yet nineteen but felt somehow ancient, eternal, in the worst possible way. My mother encouraged me to join the Arts Council and audition for two musicals. I landed two great roles. In *Showboat*, I played Julie, the half-caste singer, and sang "Can't Help Lovin' That Man of Mine" as well as the haunting blues number "Bill." In *Sweethearts*, I was cast as the soubrette, Liane. I was a great success, and for the first time in my life, I felt truly myself, when I was performing. It was also the first time I can remember my mother being proud of me.

A wealthy young farmer from Firefly fell in love with me during *Showboat* and even approached my parents to ask if he could become engaged to me. That's how strangely things always seemed to happen in my life.

Eventually, the doctors gave me permission to finish my scholarship. I returned to college, completed my final semester, and graduated. Everyone believed I would be safe as a teacher.

We later learned from the Kingsford police that the woman who had thrown me out, her name was Nita Rhu, was well known to them. She had done the same thing to several young girls over the years, always advertising rooms in the back pages of the *Catholic Weekly*.

Surely you can see that with so much happenstance in my young life, the remembering is exhausting. It often demands long intervals of rest, and swimming at my safe place, in the salt air.

As I wade into the sea now, it feels almost animal, pounding and beating against my skin and heart. Once I push through the shore

## Next Foot Forward

dump, it becomes something tender. With gentle fingers, it cradles and rocks me, gliding softly along my skin. Finally, I float, eyes closed to the sky, listening as the sea whispers to the sand. The ocean is my refuge, the one place where my legs feel safe.

Sometimes my selfishness surprises me. Like this morning, when I went down to swim. There wasn't a soul in sight, not even a dog. The surface of the pool was stretched taut like a full sail, gleaming with that autumn sheen. It reminded me of polished silicon.

All mine. No human noise. Mine to make the first mark on the morning.

It isn't easy swimming in winter's approach. I walk down barefoot so a part of me is already cold, ready, accepting. I like my mind to challenge my body.

Unfortunately, my mind never seemed to find its way into boys, dating, or marriage, not even into music or fashion, really.

I graduated without attending the ceremony, which infuriated my mother, who had travelled four hundred kilometres for the occasion. The thought of receiving a piece of paper, shaking a hand, and dressing in that old-fashioned gown and cap felt insulting to my mind, so I simply didn't go.

You might well wonder, dear marathon readers who've stayed with me this far, how I ever got married or had the child I've already spoken of earlier in my story.

I was now a freshly minted twenty-year-old teacher, living independently but always returning to this beach for every holiday. A group of young men from the city used to rent a place here each January, and as this was still a small coastal hamlet, we all knew each other. They owned a ski boat, and often a group of us would water-ski on the nearby river. I loved that, it was one of the few sports where my legs weren't at risk.

## Adelina Basile

In typical Australian fashion, each summer the same people gathered, swam, and socialised. I felt lucky to be part of it, though my brothers were always among the group too.

One of the boys, Ron, went to my father, unbeknownst to me, and asked for permission to marry me. I can only assume my father thought that marriage, or at least dating, must have already been discussed between us. He said yes.

Ron was a nice enough boy, four years older than I, and a builder from Sydney. I had just turned twenty and was still very much an outsider in the world and its ways. What I remember most about Ron were his deep-set blue eyes beneath a strong, protruding brow, and a sharp nose that peeled each year from sunburn. He was quiet and watchful, the sort of man who played rugby union for his local club.

Thinking back, I must have been such a problem for my mother in every way, they were probably grateful. They may have even paid him! It was a time in the family fraught with worry. Too many things were happening all at once, and I can imagine my parents were relieved to have me off their hands. My nana had come to live with us for reasons I didn't yet know, and my brother Philip was in a coma at St Vincent's Hospital following a car accident. He had lost one eye and was still in a critical condition.

Docile and confused, I agreed to whatever was said. I was conscious that I was an enormous problem for my mother, and that my father was unable to support me emotionally. On top of that, our dog had a huge litter of puppies, and the household was completely unmanageable. My brother was dearly loved, the golden child, and we were all devastated by his accident.

I had never been alone with Ron, but when he came and said my father had given permission for us to marry, I simply agreed. How I came to be married without ever choosing a dress, a church, or a reception venue is testament to how truly off-key I was. I still feel ashamed just writing and remembering it.

## Next Foot Forward

I was married on a Saturday, I think, in a large church at Randwick.

The reception unfolded like theatre. To my mind it was opulent, surreal, and entirely unrehearsed. I believe my mother must have revelled in the drama and splendour of it all. The Carlton Ritz shimmered in the late afternoon light, its polished floors echoing with the laughter of strangers dressed like prosperity. Sydney's skyline loomed beyond the walls, a silent witness to a celebration that had very little to do with me.

Inside, the reception was a symphony of excess, but to my mother's perfect taste. Ice glistened like diamonds. A skilled sculptor had carved lobsters from frozen water; they perched regally on silver trays, while nude female ice figures, eerily lifelike, stood sentinel with outstretched arms, bearing offerings of oysters still nestled in their jagged shells. It was almost Greco-Roman decadence reimagined by a wealthy Australian committee that knew how to throw a party.

I'm sure it was a beautiful evening for everyone else, although I can only remember asking for a glass of milk. I was still a girl who had no voice. The catering painted a baroque and colourful picture against the sweep of white linen.

I stood in the middle of it all, dressed in ivory silk that clung to my slender frame, a body too tense for celebration. A single camellia nestled in my dark hair, as if trying to lend grace to my unease. In my hand was a cold glass of milk. No champagne flutes, no sparkling toast, just milk, white, plain, unpretentious. It suited me.

The only photo I have from that day holds a curious stillness. I am alone in it, captured in profile, a glass of milk in my right hand and a blur of colourful people in the background.

The morning after our wedding night, I was back at my parents' house, pleading to be "unmarried." My new husband had been drunk and brutal. I was a virgin, untouched before that night, and he took no notice of my pleas or pain, he raped me safely within the bounds of marriage. Mother stood at the door, blocking my way inside. She assumed I was having another nervous breakdown. The door was closed, and I was sent back to face my fearsome fate.

There was much ugliness and cruelty in that marriage, and some sexual savagery so severe that I had to see an out-of-town doctor to have my body repaired. All I knew about sex was what my mother had told me after the wedding: *"Just do everything to make your husband happy."* I do not wish to revisit the darkness of that relationship. I had lost ownership of my own body and was incapable of reacting in any useful way.

That cruel brutality resulted in my first child, and the doctors said he would not live long. *"Try to have another one quickly,"* was their advice. Seeing a frail, suffering child unravels me even now. My son Simon could not eat, gained no weight, and slept endlessly.

Five local GPs told me, and my mother, who often accompanied me, that I was *"just a nervous new mother."* In those days, you needed a referral to see a specialist, but all the doctors denied me one. So, early one morning, I packed the car, my baby, and myself, and drove to the Royal Alexandra Hospital for Children in Camperdown, Sydney.

For hours I sat and waited, pleading to see a paediatrician. Eventually, I was taken to a room and met Dr Stuckey, who, thankfully, was willing to listen. The moment he picked Simon up in his arms, he knew something was terribly wrong with his heart, even before using the stethoscope. Simon was admitted immediately, and I took my other baby to my aunt's place while we awaited the results.

There were three serious congenital abnormalities in Simon's heart, and he was also allergic to lactose and sucrose. There was

## Next Foot Forward

no surgical procedure available, and his life expectancy was between four and seven years, if we were lucky.

I was sent home with that news. The days that followed were grim, as my husband ignored all the work involved in caring for our sick child and blamed the entire situation on my side of the family.

Adelina Basile

# Chapter 13

Gazing across the ocean right now, I think it is a wonderful metaphor for change. Whales go north to mate and calve, then cruise back south with their babies; dark clouds of whitebait roil their way into our bays and out again; glimpses of large silver predators herd the baitfish like border collies; a sudden cold current cramps my legs, and on a fat tide, when the swell is from the south, I am able to hitch this body of mine onto a great glossy wave and feel it trundling beneath me, silent and strong, until I am beached on the wet sand.

This great sea of mine claims and offers at the same time. It soothes my body and my soul as I swim under the shadow of the two sea eagles who twist and turn, creating their symphony of grace and power high above the headland. They love to ride the thermals just as I love to ride a wave.

Right now, the sea has been bullied quite flat by the wind, which has changed direction and now blows from the west. I suspect that a few adventurous mullet and tailor are the shapes I see in the lips of the waves. The water is bronze, and over on the rocks, I can see children exploring the tide pools, their silhouettes backlit in this magical light. Some of the inhabitants of those tide pools have remained unchanged all my life. At least the same species seem to live in their own type of pool forever. Poking a gentle finger into the tiny, delicate feelers of a sea anemone is to taste a delicious frisson of your nerve endings. Such a sensuous experience! One year, when we were isolated because of chickenpox, my brother and I made friends with a regular octopus. Cephalopods are incredibly evolved and able to learn. She recognised the difference between us and would climb all the way up our arms, putting her head under our chins. One afternoon we took her back to the shack with us, and it was obvious she was not afraid. We had to take her back to her pool after our family meal and before the rosary was said. In the days before everyone became reactive, there were sensible rules about nature: if it is brightly coloured, it is probably

## Next Foot Forward

venomous; if it tastes sour, it is probably poisonous; and if you move a rock, put it back when you leave, it might be someone's home. These few rules served us well, and I learnt to cherish the environment that I love so dearly.

Once, long before I was born, a great humpback whale died in this bay and was washed onto the shore. It lay alone and huge halfway around the beach. My father said that even the farmers' tractors could not move it, and the Shire had to bring in heavy machinery to tow it away. They dragged it a long way, along the beach, over the dune, through the lagoon that was much wider in those days, and finally into the bush. I considered that a thoughtless act, as back then, foxes and packs of dogs roamed through this place. I feel for that whale, which should have been left on the cool sand and not dragged harshly and without dignity to a lonely place in the scrub.

My husband, a builder, worked hard. Our day started early, and I normally set the table and cooked breakfast by seven o'clock. I had always packed his lunch and thermos, and once he was gone, and before the boys were born, I went off to Taree Primary School for my day's work. Ron had always been a beer drinker ever since I had known him, but after Simon was born, he would arrive home from work already full of beer and bitterness. He was drinking heavily and seemed to be forever angry, and at the end of the day he would return sullen and cruel. He would do cruel things like purposely dropping something heavy on my foot. Once, I went to get into my car to go to work, but it just wouldn't start, and I had to catch a bus. That afternoon, he almost bragged that he had taken the starter motor out of my engine.

Life dragged my boys and me through a constant war for the next three years. Once Damian was born, I gave up my job, as there was no way I could cope with the many demands made by one sick child and a newborn baby. I received no help when Simon was ill or Damian was teething, and the constant trips to Sydney to the Children's Hospital were taking their toll on me. After a particular

## Adelina Basile

day when he threw his heavy beer tankard and almost hit Damian's head, I gathered up my courage, packed a bag and the children, and left that house of violence and abuse. There were no safe houses back in those early seventies. At first, I landed at my parents', begging them to let us stay there. "What will people think?" shouted my mother.

As it was evening, we were allowed in, but my mother said we could only stay there if my husband was there too. She sent my father to get him. For one night we existed in horrible silence while my insides were shrieking for security and relief. My parents witnessed his anger and violence when Ron punched their wall and made a hole in the plasterboard.

With no other option, I got a taxi the next morning to take us to the railway station, bought our tickets, and went to Sydney on a train. To be precise, my mother would have given me a roof over my head if I had agreed to give her my boys to be raised by her. I did not even consider this. I was quite homeless as well as jobless but had great faith that I would find a job and a place for us to live down in the city. At least there, we were close to the Children's Hospital, and Simon would be close to help, while my toddler, Damian, would be safe from any more violence or anger.

The instruction book on my life was very one-dimensional. I had to write it as I went, and it certainly lacks finesse. You just go quietly forward and find joy in insignificant things.

I let my thoughts surge inward, Reader.

For a while, I am taking myself away from that dreadful chapter of my life. Nature renews me. In my world, I talk to trees. I listen to them. The grandeur and dignity of a tree are such breathtaking things, they keep me humble. It is a perfect city. Leaning back against a Norfolk pine tree, I let my gaze wander across the grass and along the shoreline, where seaweed lies exposed at low tide. It seems I have a totem, a small, glinty-eyed male willy wagtail who appears to demand that I ask his permission before setting

## Next Foot Forward

foot on what is clearly his beach. A bird is another spark of joy. Imagine being able to move just one feather out of so many, purely for direction. A thought like that undoes me.

There is no time wasted watching the stars go by. Do you do it? Do you not long to be out there? I want to stride from star to star, naked and free in the moonlight, and declare ownership of the world in which I dare to dream. I would invite comets to follow my footsteps like phosphorescent trails obeying my feet. I want to be pulled into a wave and fly through foam in an underwater world. I want sand in my hair and seaweed winding softly around my skin. These are desires deep within me.

Reality was of a different kind. I knew I could bear pain, but I needed to become like steel. I vowed that my children would never see me downtrodden or depressed, and decided their lives should be an adventure. Without dwelling on the hardship of finding a flat and finally getting a teaching position, there was always the necessity of keeping Simon breathing.

Strangers were generous about my situation, and I often had to leave my toddler, Damian, with some unfamiliar person, perhaps a neighbour in the next apartment or one of the teachers on my staff, frequently in the middle of the night as I rushed his brother back to hospital.

Life was very full but utterly exhausting once I found a full-time teaching position. I would push the pram for about an hour to a woman who looked after my children at her home, which was a ten-minute walk to my school. I didn't know there were welfare payments I could have accessed because welfare had never been discussed or needed in my family. After work, I would push them in the pram back to our small flat. By that time, we pretty much survived on vegetables and apples, while Simon needed special formula sent from America.

It was called Nutramigen and smelled dreadful. As I recall, it was an iron- and vitamin-fortified, lactose-free powder that I mixed with sterile water. That, and spinach, were his only foods for about eighteen months of life. He also couldn't receive immunisations as Damian had done.

I know I was exhausted by that life because one morning, after dropping the boys off, I collapsed in the gutter in front of my school and vomited a fair amount of blood.

I had shamed the family by leaving my marriage, and I think my brothers, who all lived in the same city, had been encouraged by my formidable mother to avoid helping me. I believe she thought I would eventually give up, go back to the country, and live by her rules.

Every Saturday morning, we would pram to the hospital for an hour while I was taught how to perform paediatric physiotherapy because Simon's lungs wouldn't clear. From then on, I had to insert a tube down his poor little nose into his lungs and suction out the mucus each morning. The real burden was knowing that Damian would suffer insecurities because I constantly had to leave him with strangers. In those days, I never once felt sad though. I read to my children; we created a made-up language and sang together.

On Sundays, I would push the pram from Leichhardt along Parramatta Road all the way to Circular Quay. Our outing was the return trip on the Manly ferry. I would then wander through Woolloomooloo, up to the fountain at Kings Cross, down William Street, and all the way back. I suppose I pushed that pram about fifty kilometres each Sunday. The pram was weatherproof, and both boys were small. I weighed 49 kilos and was probably the fittest I've ever been in my life.

# Chapter 14

I remember reading Rachel Carson many years earlier, and I paraphrase, "we humans who live in the wonder and beauty of this earth can never be truly alone." I never am. I need it as much as I need oxygen.

Sometimes this beauty that surrounds me drives me to despair. I get a sense of not quite inhabiting my own surroundings as my physical self is preened and pruned by the elements of sun, wind, rain, and salt. Shadows slicing through the sunlit dune make me gasp. For a millisecond, I think they are real beings. Returning to myself is always a shock. I think the reason I still went with my babies to Sunday Mass was for that sense of peace I found in that hour, the same peace I now feel standing in the rain by the sea.

My brother managed a large hotel on the beach at Coogee, and an apartment had become available just behind it. We had bumped into each other quite by accident one weekend, and I asked if he knew of a cheap place for me to rent. I had also bought an old pink Ford Falcon, which allowed me to drive to work and the hospital when needed. The hotel chef got to know me and would let me slip into the dining room for free meals with the boys every now and then.

The Vietnam War was raging, and the hotel had been marked for use by the US Army Special Forces, CIA, and JAG. During my free meals, I met quite a few of these servicemen. I knew they were special because my brother had to be granted permission to carry a revolver. Men like that were prone to breaking.

Many of them just wanted someone to sit on the beach with, to talk to. Some even came to my place for a cup of tea. Their nerves were so taut, they were almost visible. I doubt two weeks of R&R ever gave them much succour. I became pen pals with three of these quiet, thoughtful, and fragile men, and often wondered why they never wanted to disappear into the outback.

## Adelina Basile

Sydney and Kings Cross in those days were alive, noisy, and vibrant with life and hope. The men of SOG (Special Operations Group) were those who had to work behind enemy lines, sometimes crossing borders and fighting a silent, deadly war. They were mostly intelligence gatherers. They dropped into places unseen in the middle of the night and, I believe, suffered the highest incidence of KIA of any group in the US Army. Their daring, courage, and honesty stole a place in my heart. My own personal war somehow matched theirs, and I felt a kinship.

By 1970, Simon was really ailing and had become almost transparent. I could not accept that we were simply going to let him die, so full of hope and faith, I grabbed my only carving knife and my rosary beads and went to the hospital. Whenever I was gripped by great fear, they were the only things I reached for. I caused a fuss at the reception desk and demanded to see the cardiac surgeon. Until then, we had only dealt with the physician. Eventually, we were escorted to the surgeon's office, where I brandished both knife and rosary beads. I remember my words exactly:

"I am Lina Basile. I am not going to leave here until you say you will operate on my son!"

Fortunately, there were no tasers back then, and the doctor was sensible, vastly amused, but also interested. He asked for Simon's doctor's name and sent for his file. I still include that doctor, Professor Tim Cartmill, in my prayers to this day. In fact, we visited him last year.

He sat me down and, with all the time in the world, explained that there were so many things wrong with Simon's heart that there was no possible procedure. By that time in my life, it was unwise to tell me there was *no procedure*. Life had taught me there was only one gear, and that was forward.

Well, I told him to be creative. I urged him to ring the doctor in South Africa who was experimenting with transplants and have a chat. I convinced him that I would sign any legal papers ensuring he wouldn't be sued or lose his licence. I could see the wheels turning in his eyes, and I became excited. I said I would rather Simon died on the operating table than waste away, lethargic and so transparent that, when bathing him, you could see his liver. We all calmed down and had a cup of tea, and he promised I would hear from him. I had no phone, so it would be by letter. I skipped home feeling as if I had faced fate and demolished it.

Three days later, the letter arrived. Simon had to undergo a myriad of tests, then spend another two days learning to stay in isolation inside an oxygen tent. If that was successful, the surgeon was going to have a go at it. Thinking and writing this now fills my eyes with tears, and my whole body is one big goosebump.

Emotions are feelings, and I think that in me, they live in my body rather than my brain. I cannot separate those two parts, but here, I can give you an example of "emotion" as I see it.

It is not the quick swell of joy in my heart when I watch a dog run on the beach or a cormorant dive like a fighter jet through the ocean's surface to catch a fish. I call that "joy."

My emotion comes when I feel jealous that I never could run or ride a bike. That I could never do a sport with other kids. I longed to ride a skateboard or surfboard, to feel speed or gravity in a profound way. I hug the giant paperbark tree down in the park and watch the ants and critters that have made it their home, but how I wish I had climbed to the very top and seen the world from that special viewpoint. Emotion, for me, was the feeling that a child would never run or breathe properly until he died at an early age.

Maybe the frustrations and envy that come from my curiosity are my emotions. I do not know the feeling of anger, and in the traumatic times of my life, I am particularly grateful that I do not.

Let me be the narrator as I tell the story of my most fearsome hours in my conscious life.

## Adelina Basile

# Chapter 15

Look at me. Do I catch your interest? I am looking at myself with kindness and awe. Meet me here, in this memory I wish to share.

There was such fear and confusion swirling in bands of hope around my body. I had informed my ex-husband and his family about Simon's upcoming operation, but they never came by. I knew I would be waiting for several hours, so I dressed in a long-sleeved blouse and blue jeans. I wore a jumper, shoes, and socks because I was used to the cold, chilly currents that swept through hospital corridors, and I wanted to be prepared. In my rush to get to the hospital at five o'clock in the morning, I forgot to pack any food or drink.

He was so tiny, so very small, lying on the hospital trolley that would take him into surgery. Drowsy but awake, his clear blue eyes stunned me with their purity and beauty.

I had previously met with the surgeon, who explained,

"Lina, I know this is a lot to take in. Simon's heart surgery is delicate, but we're prepared. During the operation, we'll use a technique called hypothermic circulatory arrest. To put it simply, we'll cool his body, pack him in sterile ice until his temperature drops enough to slow his metabolism. That helps protect his brain and organs while we work.

We'll also connect him to what we call a heart-lung bypass machine. It will take over for his heart and lungs during the operation, circulating his blood and keeping it oxygenated. It gives us the stillness and time we need to repair the defects without strain on his heart.

It might sound stark, I know. But this approach, though new, gives Simon the best chance. Once everything's in place, we'll begin. And when it's done, we'll gently warm him, restart his heart, and return the function to his own lungs.

## Next Foot Forward

It's a lot to trust us with, but I promise you, we'll treat him with great care."

The doctors had discussed the surgery and decided it would be wise to limit the time on the bypass machine to forty-five minutes. Kissing him goodbye, I inhaled his sweet, milky scent and watched as he was wheeled away down the long corridor.

My mind followed Simon's journey as I slumped into a straight-backed chair and closed my eyes, fighting the enormous panic that rose within me. In my imagination, the clanging, clacking trolley carried its tiny prize through sterile whiteness into the operating theatre. That place was the essence of all things clinical, bright lights, a green-gowned cast waiting, gloved hands held high in reverence, perhaps, to this little life. I wondered how nervous the nurses and doctors were and remembered the legal papers I had signed to allow the procedure.

It was here that the world of modern science and technology would come to the fore, partnering with the surgeons' skill. It was here that the bypass machine would work efficiently, pumping blood to a brain whose body was frozen in ice and whose heart lived outside its place, held by steady hands.

We are fortunate we do not have to see it. We are victims of our own imaginings, aware of the devastation within those cells and organs. Time lost all meaning, and there were no boundaries in this space as I sat alone, panicked and prayerful. It was hard to match my breathing to the rhythm of my imagined waves.

I did not sleep, but when I finally looked at my watch, I realised fifteen hours had passed. In the distance, coming down the corridor, I saw a bent and crooked figure approaching. For a moment, I thought there might have been another waiting room where others had been sitting. As he drew nearer, I was shocked to realise it was Simon's surgeon. That young, dapper chief surgeon had been reduced to weary old age in just fifteen hours.

## Adelina Basile

"I'm sorry. His heart won't restart. We have him on life support. It is rare, but sometimes this is how the muscle of the heart reacts to the trauma of the scalpel. Visit him, and then we'll discuss turning off the machines later," he told me, weariness oozing from every pore of his greyed face. I felt terrible for him. I don't think his words registered in my brain, but I shook his hand and thanked him.

Then off I marched into the horror chamber that was the recovery room, metaphorically rolling up my sleeves, straightening my back, pulling up my socks, ready for work.

I had not expected that such a small child would be lying naked, bruised from chin to toe, in a huge room where giant machines seemed attached to every part of his exposed body. At first, they were reluctant to let me in, as it was a gory, bloody scene, but they soon saw that none of it made any difference to me.

Simon had been on the heart-lung machine for one hundred and fifteen minutes longer than recommended in this emerging field of paediatric cardiac surgery. As a result, the doctors and nurses told me that even if he survived, he would have brain damage that could be quite severe.

Damian was being looked after by my parents back in our regional town, so I stayed with Simon for about fourteen hours a day. On the floor below the Intensive Care Unit, there was a lovely little chapel where I found great solace. Many of his nurses came and prayed beside me, or simply sat talking with me after they had finished their shifts. I cannot remember what I ate or even where I slept, but on day thirteen, I was in the middle of the Joyful Mysteries of the Rosary when a nurse came, her face beaming, to tell me his heart had started to beat by itself and that he would soon be moved from recovery to the Intensive Care Unit. On the day that Simon's heart began beating on its own, I knew that whatever life's vagaries came across my path, until the day I died,

## Next Foot Forward

I would never lose faith or hope again. I felt that I was born for miracles to happen.

During the long and lonely hours sitting on a hard hospital chair waiting for that heart operation to end, I thought about taxi drivers. I wondered what it would be like to work a night shift in a city. It took my mind away from Simon as I jotted ideas on my ever-present pad.

The taxi driver of the city night: hollow man, or straw man, shadowless; denizen of invisibility. Sometimes "cabbie" or "mate" to some, nameless to others. A man of evening, a man of the night shift, clocking on after the day driver, whom I named "Zengo of the grey cardigan", finished his shift and was off to Coogee for his son's birthday. Now it is time to absorb the heat of the day trapped in the car seat. A seat too short for legs long and inclined to cramp. Ford or Holden makes no difference, cruising Bayswater or conforming to the taxi rank, he's paid his dues.

There, flagged down... hopefully a friendly one here inside the deserted darkness somewhere in this city, within the nightness of it all. A nocturnal back and forth of humanity, sometimes inhuman, but in the guise of those with money in their pockets. Perhaps he's their only few minutes of comfort or safety as they hurry about, mole-like in the burrows of the underground blackness of their lives.

And the lovers, hand-holding, touching, impatient, going to who-cares-where, borne along by Bill or John, taxi driver anonymous and automatic, taking part, unknown to them, in their flashing, searching ritual of something: a celebration of life. He's happy not to have to talk. They know what they are doing, and he's just part of the metal and machinery stage set.

Taxi ramp, harsh light, and one-thirty am with late news flash and empty streets stretching out for another four and a half hours. Thoughts of opportunities lost or missed spark and spiral in technicolour, brighter than the Dixon Street Festival lights. He's doing the sitting there out of choice, a percentage on an hourly rate.

Not caring; maybe the pedestrians wandering by need a ride. Start the engine, trusting the computer in his head. A quick U-turn to save two blocks, turning down the radio, the fare's a talker. Answering yes, or no, or perhaps, not likely, customer always right. Mind in neutral and car in third or fourth, a bit noisy, must check it out later. "The next on the left, yes, beside that garbage bin, thank you. Slam."

Alone and on your way again, almost hitting the night mongrel dog, animal, and he dreams of friends he knew, ones who had dogs, who had died, or disappeared. Because it's a slow night, he knows it's $97.80, adding it up in bits through the night.

The moon's on the sea, the city-sea. Does it gather his heart, the glory of indigo and almost silver, part of the city, yet not? Ease foot off pedal, forget the fare, getting the salt smell and easterly breeze touching the immobility of his face with memories of other moons and seas and beach night sounds, striking chords gentle and soul-plucking. But just for a moment, it's late, and he might make two more fares if he's lucky. Life is like that.

I spent long hours in my mind being a taxi driver on Simon's operation day.

Next Foot Forward

# Chapter 16

As I look back on the hours that followed the surgery, I wonder how I managed to deal with the many urgencies that arose in the days that followed. I did not feel shame or guilt about the clerical sexual abuse I endured until I was an adult, so my faith stayed strong. To this day, I am either delusional or very lucky that I have been able to keep my faith separate from the Church, and I am acutely aware that most survivors do not have that ability.

When I sit in a mass, the air seems to disappear, and my mind bursts open in an exquisite explosion of purity. I float, and my soul grows vast. I am filled with love for the entire universe.

An arborist is coming into my street tomorrow to fell a giant tallowwood eucalypt that I have known since I could walk. It stands in the yard across the road from me and is being cut down because the neighbour next door does not like shade. This is a home to a brush-tailed possum and the resting place for flocks of lorikeets that fly high above my house every summer. Like a paintbox spilled across the sky, they twist and unfurl their colours as they chatter and call their way down to the fifth pine tree, which is their next stop. There are three nests high up in the foliage, and because we humans care so little about other beings' environments, tomorrow a tree-city will be gone. Worse still, that neighbour only spends a total of three months in this village, never longer.

When Pope John Paul said, "The Earth will not continue to offer its harvest, except with faithful stewardship," he was exactly right. Our environment is now paying us back for our laziness, exponentially, I fear.

The loggers did come and kill my tree-neighbour, so while it was happening, I took my notebook and pencil to accompany me away from the shattering, shrieking, and groaning of this life cut down in its prime. Nestled deep in the dunes amid the spiky grasses, I watched a hawk high in the sky. Hawks are mostly found further inland, and I expect he could probably see and hear the cries of his eucalypt neighbour being felled. He stayed for ages, long enough for me to write a poem for him as he quartered along the surf line, where gulls and terns had squatted in the early light that cast a sheen of gold on their breasts. One gull had moved away from the rest as he dipped his beak for a worm or pipi. I called him Old Gull.

I wrote:

Predator bird of mountain air, soaring out upon the sea,

Unaware you tamper there to bring grim misery.

Oh hawk, you swift alluring bird, you glide on velvet air,

Lured on you come, but do you sense the beauty there?

This hunter stalks on swiftest wings, he scans in search of prey,

That old gull lives with quickened heart; the hawk comes to hunt that day.

The old gull knows what dangers come when the hawk invades his lair,

I can hear his mournful call through the silence of the air.

One thing I know, if I know naught else, the hawk can't stay at sea.

I see a storm about to come; this hawk must seek a tree.

There are no trees among the waves, the hawk can't really stay,

Being just a visitor that came to hunt that day.

The gull had a safer fate than my tree. They left it about three metres tall, alone, undignified, and dying.

## Chapter 17

Prior to Simon's surgery, I had to give up my job and was once more homeless. It seems wrong to say I had no friends, but life had not given me time to make them, and truthfully, I never thought about any kind of social life. It was obvious that I would have to move back home and hopefully out to our beach shack, which was not used much because everyone was working away in the cities. My boys needed clean air, stability, and time to simply be alive without the turmoil that had surrounded them for so many years. I did, however, enjoy a deep and interesting friendship with one of my American pen pals from earlier. His name was Richard, and through our correspondence, we discovered that we understood each other. He had proposed to me by mail at the time when Simon was in post-surgery. I gave it no thought, as I had never considered marriage in any situation. My life already seemed full to the brim with everything that was happening. Besides, I knew nothing about military matters.

I knew that no one was living at the beach shack, so I very hopefully approached my mother.

"Mother, do you think we could live out at the beach until Simon recovers and I am able to find a job?"

She barely raised her head from the coloured wool she was crocheting. "How are you going to support yourself? You have done nothing but bring shame to the family." This conversation took place while my father was at work, as I felt terrible having to beg. I didn't want him to see me being refused, in case it made him upset with my mother. And I had no answer for her.

I do not know why I was such a burden to her. I was kind and honest, clean, clever, and frugal, but some part of me angered her. Years later, when I discovered I was autistic, I thought that might have been the reason, but it truly made no sense because I had managed through life in what I considered a very successful manner. There is no point wondering about that now because her next decision overcame me.

"On condition that you give me the boys to raise as I think fit," came the unexpected sentence from her grim mouth. We had no eye contact at all. Bewildered, I tried to ask for time out at the beach shack, at least until Simon was healed. Our conversation dwindled to silence.

I promptly forgot about it, because during the weeks after surgery I was very busy giving Simon exercise, keeping his large chest wound clean, and making sure Damian was included in everything we did. I taught them the card game of canasta, and we spent many hours on the floor playing that or Uno. I was too busy trying to keep my children safe to think of any other kind of life.

Today is a grey, mysterious one here at my beach. A salty mist hangs low along the shore, and maybe winter has decided to tease us with a lick or two. My laptop and I are halfway along the beach, tucked into a hollow under a roosting tree for the sea eagles. Two of my pet dogs are buried here, Storm Boy and Nimbus. They were big, black, blue-tongued Chow dogs interested in no other animal. I was their only human. Storm Boy could master the look of affront and disdain better than any dog, or human. Naturally, my two black-headed sea eagles have these names. I think that is fitting. I say that because there is another pair of sea eagles over along Back Beach. They roost above a huge casuarina tree and show off their speed and tricks high above the headland. They are the ones I watch as I swim.

I found a small pilot whale early yesterday morning, lying dead on the sand while the gum trees behind the dune were shedding their bark. Last night I sat under the autumn moon, full and heavy (the moon and my heart alike), and watched a high-velocity star burst out into space, far away from the moon. It was a force of nature sharing a vast secret with me, under that fat, full moon.

## Next Foot Forward

Ah. I have had severe and crippling panic attacks ever since I became a single parent trying to support two little boys, so, we can say for at least fifty years. I am pretty much confined to this extraordinarily beautiful little beach because I do not seem to have trust. I believe everything that is said to me and am aware that I have no filter to avoid the dross, but I have never had anyone to trust but myself, not in people, railway lines, professions, councils… pretty much everything man-made or managed. I am only secure with nature. This is where I belong. I have an acute sense of bush smell and could tell you where a snake passed by in the night. I trust myself and the natural environment.

My diagnosis (and I am not sure I trust it) is PTSD plus Complex Trauma. From my point of view, as I see our climate beginning to destroy us, many people must be like me, with the planet in such a state of agony. It is just a pity I cannot ever find them. Anyway, none of us would probably trust each other! My safest place is the ocean.

The pounding sea is often in my dreams, and its mists pour and swirl around me. The silvery sphere of the moon prevails, pulling upon my shore on those special nights. When the moon hides in the troughs and rides the wave crests, it crushes all my hopes and dreams to sand and empties me relentlessly. Then I am fresh all over again. I wrote a poem for my seabirds, who are both love and hope, curling tightly around my desperate spirit.

**THE SEA BIRDS (Love and Hope)**

*The chains that hold a seabird to the ground,*

*Can they long be shackled*

*about his tiny feet?*

*Feet meant to run on sandy shores*

*or the beach of time eternal.*

## Adelina Basile

*You have not heard of chains upon a bird?*

*But surely, this must be so.*

*Have you never walked the beach of time,*

*gazed out upon its endless seas?*

*And were there, at times,*

*no seabirds there?*

*They are perhaps shackled to the ground,*

*The chains of heartbreak,*

*A burden beyond the will to fly.*

*It is also true that some may die,*

*For can you take away the flight of such a bird*

*Who knows only*

*The freedom of the air flowing over wings of gold and silver,*

*The surf of happiness, the tides of destiny*

*Sliding to and fro*

*Under his watchful eye?*

*He must surely die.*

*But there is a key,*

*A key of life*

*to unlock the bonds of death.*

*It is hope.*

*For hope is love,*

**Next Foot Forward**

*The seabird's song.*

*Is anything so free*

*as the birds*

*that sail along the sea?*

*Is there not life, special, beautiful,*

*sailing there on intrepid wings?*

*I shall find my strength in the seabird's song.*

*I shall loose the bonds of all the birds I find,*

*Destined there to death no more.*

*I love the seabirds,*

*And when I look out on the sea of time,*

*There,*

*sailing in their greatest majesty,*

*They shall call to me, a song of hope,*

*A song of love.*

# Chapter 18

The circumstances of my life with my first husband were so extreme that I was an exception to the law requiring people to wait seven years before they could be divorced. I was fortunate because there was so much factual evidence that I obtained the divorce just a year after escaping that stultifying and terrifying situation. I remember the Catholic Church tribunal, which consisted of three priests in the same diocese where I had been so sexually abused, seemed quite unsurprised at my request. As I realise now, they were probably quite aware of Father Denis. Interestingly, the leader of the annulment tribunal was a Fr Vince Ryan, who was later convicted and sentenced to a long jail term for sexual abuse. My marriage was annulled on the grounds of insufficient understanding of marriage.

Richard, my pen pal and admirer, the sometimes CIA operative, did secret things in faraway, classified places. I had first met him three years prior, in Sydney. It was then that we exchanged names and addresses and vowed to write to each other. After he signed up for a third tour in Vietnam, he was granted a month's R and R (rest and recreation) in Sydney. He spent his leave at my brother's hotel again, and we became familiar and friendly, first with me and the boys, and gradually with my parents and siblings. My brother often brought some of the Green Berets up for a few days at our beach.

The night I best remember was the evening my brother and his wife took us out to dinner. I was in the city, restlessly awaiting Simon's discharge from his hospital scans, when they invited me along. I remember wearing a green silk halter-neck dress with a skimpy skirt, in the fashion of the hot pants era of the seventies. We danced while the live band played *Spanish Eyes*. He was average in height, quiet, polite, with dark hair, and had a face and attitude that tuned in and listened. It might have been the first time someone had paid attention to my thoughts and words. He asked questions. He told me how much he loved the men of his A-team,

## Next Foot Forward

for whom he was responsible, and introduced me to the fascinating history of the indigenous hill people of Vietnam, called the Montagnards. I may have fallen in love with him at that very moment, because when I look back on that night, I can't remember a thing about my brother or his wife. That night, and our letters, which came and went via an APO military address somewhere in California, was the extent of *us*.

We had become great friends through our letters, and he had talked about coming to Australia to visit again. He warned me that he couldn't share much about his work, and I wasn't particularly curious about the army anyway. After he was promoted to Captain, he wrote while recovering from a bullet wound. My mother was beside me as she handed me the letter and was aware of his proposal.

"My dearest Lina,

I have had time to assess my life as I wait for this wound to heal. (I think he had a bit of shrapnel in him.) We get along so well, and I would love to help you raise your boys. Would you consider marriage?

At present, I am in Thailand but have decided to re-up for another six-month tour. Because I have time on my hands, I've begun the paperwork in the hope that you will accept me. Hoping to hear from you, positively and with love,

Richard

P.S. I've lost weight due to a bad case of malaria."

I cheerfully and politely rejected his proposal of marriage and gave it no further thought. My energies were exhausted by the simple day-to-day responsibilities of motherhood and the extremely tense relationship with my mother. However, just five weeks after I had refused his proposal, I was told one afternoon by my mother to go to the airport to meet him! Somehow, my mother had sent a telegram, in the middle of the Vietnam War, to a secret operative saying, *"Come down. The marriage is on. She just had wedding jitters."* The enormity of that maternal act still leaves me speechless.

At first, I didn't believe her. How would anyone even know how to do that?

"Don't let us look bad in this town. The plane arrives tonight."

"Father," I pleaded, "please go to him and explain that it's all a mistake."

His eyes couldn't meet mine. He hunched his shoulders, looking defeated.

"Your mother and I think this might be the answer to your problem. You have nowhere to live and a recovering child and toddler."

I couldn't hurt him further, as I knew that once again, he had been defeated by the force of my mother. He and I had no way of standing up to her.

A panic attack, and the fear it evokes, is, as Dr Claire Weekes says, "greater than any the average person has known, or has paused to imagine." It truly is. You feel as though you are going forward towards dying. My mind would freeze, and all I could do was try to ride the wave of fear and breathlessness. It hurt that my parents didn't, even once, consider my needs or desires. The fact that I really wasn't wanted, valued, or supported cut into my heart, and still hurts me now.

The relentless tenacity deep inside my mother still amazes me to this day.

Just recently, while working my way through therapy, I became both upset and amused when my therapist/social worker said, *"Your mother pimped you!"*

## Chapter 19

My father handed me the car keys.

"Take the car. Richard is flying in on the eight p.m. flight."

I drove off into the night to the airport, which in those days was busy with flights. Again, for me, there was no other way but to step forward. I simply couldn't find choices or options. So, I nervously waited at the tarmac to greet him as my future husband.

The next week flew by in a blur. Someone on my father's cousin's side was high up in the Registry Office, and my mother, without my knowledge, had ordered a Julie Jones two-piece summer suit in pale blue for me to wear to the civil wedding that I had not discussed with anyone.

My first marriage had been organised by others too, as I hadn't chosen the church, gown, reception venue, or even the guests. The same old thing was happening all over again, only now I had two small children and was suddenly aware that I would have to leave my country, my town, and my beach. I can't imagine the amount of paperwork an American man serving in the U.S. Army would have filed for permission to marry an Australian. Especially one on active duty within SOG (Special Operations Group) during the Vietnam War.

Like a wave forced to push itself onto the shore and find rest, I determined to go forward with optimism and love, and hopefully find some peace.

Richard and I were married on a summer day at the Registry Office in Sydney and spent our first married night at a cinema watching a war movie. The final two weeks of his leave were spent on this very stretch of sand, in our beach shack. We simply agreed that I, who had no idea of military life, could choose to live and do as I pleased. He made sure I understood that he would have to come and go unexpectedly, and that I could never know where or why.

## Adelina Basile

He adored serving his country and was already a captain. His chest was full of honours, stars and oak leaves, purple hearts, and bright colours.

For a long while, I hadn't meant to be seen.

The room had been mine, a den built from silence and order, where everything stayed clean, untouched. Safe. Until Richard crashed in uninvited, cracking the walls with a smile that knew too much.

His body was firm, yes, but it was his eyes that reached through like warm hands dipped in honey. The knight. The storybook. All those fragile fantasies I thought I'd sealed away.

Love didn't arrive with flowers. It came with a purple heart.

It cut me, deep and bloody, before I could even whisper *wait*.

The air vanished. Time folded in on itself.

It was just us. I didn't need to wait.

No gravity. No bone. No breath.

His touch was the kind you don't recover from, not because it bruised, but because it didn't.

I'd known hands before. Hands that violated, slapped, pressed me into silence.

But this was different. And it made me dissolve. We flayed each other open without knowing why.

Undid the skins we had both worn to survive. Became transparent, ectoplasmic, terrifyingly real. I had never touched someone with my heart before, never been touched without a cost.

But here we were, almost bloodless and boneless, yet still somehow alive.

## Next Foot Forward

In the distance, I see a couple. They are walking hand in hand along the beach, and I am jealous. I have walked hand in hand. It is a gesture of something that is often habit... or perhaps a way to balance... or to avoid having to talk in words. *Hand in hand.*

The consideration is the body language, the spacing of the footprints and where the chins are pointing. I think of my lost and only love, Richard. My hand in hand would never be close enough to your warmth, to the truths that fall from you as your eyes grow dark in intrigue and independence.

I would rather cut wrists or fingers and share a bloody bond than walk hand in hand with shoulders pointed away.

Our shoulders inclined together, and it was warm and right, with honest hearts and truthful eyes, that night before you had to go.

If ever we were found again and walked hand in hand, I would run behind us every mile to ensure that my left footprint was well inside your right one... that we were once again three-legged.

Readers, my children are unaware of the childishness of their mother, and I write without fear because their interests lie either on top of or under the ocean, so I can be frank.

Another winter is almost over, and the weeds and their flowers are struggling their way through the cracks of the tarred track that runs along the edge of the beach and into our parks. The first to appear are wild weeds, not unlike dandelions, with bright yellow petals.

Yellow, bright, light yellow, is my favourite colour. The colour you see deep inside a flower's head. It's a colour that reaches my heart and turns it soft.

As a three-year-old, I loved colour so much that I ate the deadly yellow anther of our lily and burnt out my oesophagus. To this day, I choke a great deal for no reason, and during one of my panic attacks, I choke and burn that yellow all over again.

## Adelina Basile

An aunt of mine once said that I *tasted* colour. It's possible, my mother once found me sitting on the front path of our house in town, and I had somehow managed to eat a very bright green tree frog, except for some guts and one rear leg, which she managed to save.

I can see her shadow on the path as she bent over me, the sun hot on my head and under my legs. There was a wasp nest in the palm tree above the path, and they made movement in the air.

These days, as a practising artist, I seem to fight with colour and have greatly reduced my palette as I heave paint across my canvases.

Yesterday, the ocean pool at the southern end of my beach shimmered in the sun like a silky grey coverlet. It was a day full of birds. They floated and glided above me as I swam in the pool. They placed their shadows beneath me. There, in the neck of the headland, I watched them as they played, fought, and communicated among themselves.

For most of my life, I have loathed the colour black and refused to wear it. It always reminds me of the priest's suit. For some reason, known only to stars and sages, the sky above me was filled with feathered things, large and small, and all black.

There was the small black cormorant, like a fighter plane, rushing up to the majestic male sea eagle, which stood out as the only non-black creature in the sky above me. He was pushed away, warned off, the eagle demanding space. I recognise that feeling well. Space is imperative for thinking, resting, and healing.

The smaller female eagle, Nimbus, had more sense and took off towards the horizon, enjoying the occasional updrafts that carried her, weightless, up and up, a tiny black speck in the sky.

Pied cormorants started diving into the ocean in a feeding frenzy. A ball of baitfish was rolling along, heading north, just a shadow

## Next Foot Forward

under the surface. Every few minutes, the light would glint across the fish as they jumped and broke through the water.

I floated on my back, feeling so privileged in this wonderful seasonal window, a few weeks before tourists would arrive, and their voices would shatter this silence. More black creatures flew in a kind of unstructured convoy around the rocks of the headland. I have never seen so many crows all in one day, all cawing and probably reciting poetry in their own language. We all know how very clever they are.

My eyes followed them, and I was led to the welcome swallows, twittering and darting in jerky little swoops under the concrete awning of the surf club's veranda. The last time so many busy animals had overwhelmed me, I had been snorkelling in these waters one afternoon when suddenly fish, sand, seaweed, crabs, and sea urchins all came hurtling straight towards my mask. It was an eerie experience. I heard later that Newcastle had been hit by an earthquake and the city had been badly damaged.

That thought crossed my mind, but I was drowsy with peace and warmth, and far too relaxed to worry. Still, there were layers of birds. The magpie-larks, or peewees, friendly, inquisitive creatures, came by like a black-and-white marching band across the edge of the pool. They ventured onto the rockpools looking for food, I think.

Floating on my back, suspended by the salt water, I recognised that my heart was open and full of this pleasure. What a remarkable gift Gaia had given me in this, my daily swim.

As I dragged myself out of the water, there were my two friendly little wagtails, always there, ever friendly and composed, obviously waiting for my thanks. I have begun to think of them as my totem, as I am forever asking their permission to pass onto the sand or go to the water. I have never been able to find where they live.

## Adelina Basile

There were so many crows yesterday, and I am wondering what the weather has in store for us in the next few days.

This was the beach, the part of Australia that Richard had agreed to move to when he left the army. It was the place where we learned about each other while wandering around the rocks and sitting in the bat cave. They were insectivorous bats, tiny ones. We swam together in the natural rockpool beyond the cave. It seemed as if we shared a double-sided skin.

We explored the small rockpools, poking our fingers into the soft tentacles of the sea anemones as I pointed out the resident octopus, which was changing colour before our eyes. We were an ancient crossword puzzle of storylines, already completed. He taught me sex, and I taught him sharing, and we gave each other love.

We had the same thought at the same time. Our morbid humour was shared, and we shone with pride as we smiled at each other over the heads of two very happy little boys. He was already a hero to them. They were entranced by the stories Richard told them about his job, the glory bits boys loved: guns, weapons, underwater mines, and HALO jumping in the blackest of nights. He was able to show pride in his achievements while totally avoiding the ugliness of warfare.

I experienced the saddest, most melancholic feeling that pushed my heart further around my ribs as we flew over the Northern Territory and I looked down at my great brown and empty homeland. My bones seemed to turn to jelly, and my breath was long in coming back into my lungs as I turned my eyes, now full of tears, back over the clouds down south.

I wanted peace and stability, clean air, and fresh food for my boys. We had managed to get through four years of turmoil and abandonment. There had never been someone to back me up for as long as I could remember in my twenty-six years, and as I sat beside my brand-new husband, I felt that maybe, for a while, I could relax just a little.

## Next Foot Forward

Those children of mine had never given me a moment of trouble, and while the doctors would have preferred that Simon live close to a big hospital, I accepted that I was a huge burden to my family. I felt that the boys deserved some freedom, to be children, without the pall of hospital or the demands of my family looming over them.

Anyway, it was a moot point, as I was homeless, jobless, and now married again, and not my family's problem anymore.

Nothing had prepared me for the thoughtfulness of Richard, who had organised my living arrangements on the island of Okinawa. A house overlooking the East China Sea was our first home until he was given officers' quarters. If I smell teak oil, hibiscus scent, or salted fish to this day, I am transported back to that island of sweet, warm air that I came to love.

Suddenly, I had a house full of proper and beautiful furniture. My children had cosy beds with colourful futon doonas. Simon's coverlet was pink, while Damian's was bright yellow. Best of all, there was a part of the Pacific Ocean close by, so there would be the freedom that only a coastline, or beach, can afford me.

## Chapter 20

Early this morning, I went across the road to visit the tree they killed. This is a slow and painful death, and hard to watch. The trunk stands proud, three metres tall, and weeping. As I embrace it, there is a noticeable difference in its warmth, and I can no longer hear the humming and bustling when I press my ear close. Great swathes of thick bark cling desperately to the shiny orange cambium, pieces so huge you could make a raft from one.

Trees and oceans, birds and all creatures are part of me. It's not something I was ever taught; I've known it since I was tiny. I hurt when they do. We have mutual respect. When I catch a fish for dinner, I thank its soul for the nourishment it provides. I hurt when people hurt too, but there is rarely any reciprocity, so I am often depleted by the human side of things.

After speaking to the dying tree at sunrise, I walked along the shore, my footsteps following like a faithful puppy as there were no others around. The sunrise gilded the sand and the water, stretching out to a molten horizon. The sea breeze had not yet woken, and the air left a soft mist on my skin. My heart refuelled, and warmth trickled into my worrying blood vessels, spreading happiness until I could have melted with love. The feeling of being part of all this beauty and honest natural energy once more defined my sense of being.

Both my dogs were close beside my heels. They are rescued Italian Greyhounds, both from traumatic lives and, as a result, the timidest dogs I have ever shared my life with. In the many places I've lived, I've always had a dog as part of our family.

The great black Chow, called Storm Boy, who is buried in the dune under the sea eagles' roost, was my protector when I tried to live organically on some acres along the road. I had to work as well during the eighties. This was when Simon's heart was again

## Next Foot Forward

causing trouble, and we were back from overseas. I was prone once more to nervous collapses and panic fits.

The driveway to the carport was a few hundred metres of winding dirt track. It was a joy to come home from work to the indomitable Storm Boy. The dog knew when I was due home (I think). As I drove up the dirt track, he was always there, a black mound of fur, mute and myopic, standing on four straight legs in the characteristic Chow stance. He didn't react in any ecstatic way; the lolling tongue and wagging tail syndrome of man's best friend was not manifested in my pet.

Rather, he faced the car front-on so I was forced to a halt. He then turned, power steering, no inch given, and surveyed the dirt ahead. I waited as he slowly, majestically, picked his way through the minefield of the last fifty metres. He would spy a goose wandering lost from the flock in the tall grass on the verge. One ear pricked up (the other ear is a story for another chapter), a signal that reminded me of a military, medal-laden captain leading an advance party through no man's land.

We froze. I watched the goose's head see-sawing through the tall autumn grass. The dog watched too. We waited. He deemed it safe. He led off while I tried to contain the melting ice cream in the brown paper bag, I'd bought on my way home for the boys and me each day. The urge to abandon the car and race to the front door, to sanity, always grew strong at this point.

I sighed and accepted the gift of my homecoming ceremony. One more sweep around the lemon trees and I'd be in the garage. But wait!

The pale cat, always on the roof, was padding past the trees. It was not supposed to be there. The canine Holmes had noticed. All was not right at 3:55 p.m. at 5 Blackhead Road. That cat shouldn't be there. The black cat, maybe, he sometimes waited behind the chopping block to pounce on the dog's back foot, but not this pale one.

## Adelina Basile

Harmony shattered; routine fractured. We stopped again. *Why don't you chase the thing?* I'd think in misery. *To what god of animals did you pledge your vow of silence, of stillness?*

A Chow of the contemplative order of canines.

Bark, dog! Skit, cat! Chase!

But no.

In the centre of my driveway, in perfect alignment with the Subaru insignia, he stood, ramrod straight, my guardian. I tried going around this black sentinel of my virtue and welfare. He shuffled, a sidestep as adroit as that of a youthful Pelé. The pale cat stopped too. They stared. I think their gazes met at some invisible point in the centre of that space. How do they communicate through the heavy air of my despair?

A silent détente. In instant accord, they moved. The cat, tail high with a slice of tongue curled up, headed off while the dog went forward.

Ah! The carport loomed close. He high-stepped daintily, like a Santa reindeer, over the half-inch concrete lip. My two front wheels rolled up and over, and the car drifted to a halt. He wandered to my door, his goofy mouth smiling as always. Then suddenly his legs buckled, and he plonked to the ground to scratch his haunch.

Impossible for me to open the door, I'd butt-crawl across the gear stick, half fall out the passenger door, and drag myself inside with my schoolbooks, work bag, groceries, and melting ice cream.

Each school day that was my greeting from Storm Boy, and I have as many stories about dogs as the twenty-seven dogs I have given homes to in my life. Dogs are my people too, like trees and oceans. They have the capacity to refill me.

### Next Foot Forward

Right now, I wish I had access to the weekly letters I wrote to my parents religiously every Sunday night. I filled pages with descriptions of Okinawan colours and sounds, our activities, and how the military worked. I had hoped one day my sons would be able to read of their young life experiences through those fulsome letters. I even sketched in them.

After five years away from home, when I did return, it was to discover that my mother had burned or thrown away my letters. Saddest of all was realising that no one else in the family had thought to keep them for me.

If you can hear me swallow, dear reader, it's because big, fat tears are trying to come out of my eyes, and I'm snorting them down my throat.

Aside from my letters, everything precious I had left packed carefully in my parents' garage had been given away, lost, or destroyed. No one in my family was ever able to tell me what had happened.

It's why, even today, I have only four mugs, three glasses, and a sad amount of cutlery. I do miss all the awards I'd won for art and writing that I'd submitted to the *Sunday Herald* children's pages from the time I was five.

Adelina Basile

# Chapter 21

Okinawa is a subtropical island and the largest of the Ryukyu chain. It is tiny from an Australian perspective, one hundred and six kilometres long and about eleven kilometres wide. Flying into it for the first time is terrifying. From the air, it seems there isn't enough land for the plane, and you'll surely end up landing somewhere in the ocean.

It was where one of the most decisive battles was fought at the end of World War Two, and more than one hundred thousand Japanese soldiers died there. It's common for an unexploded mine or bomb to be discovered, often by children. The civilian population was also decimated during the war, and the hills surrounding the cities and towns are dotted with beautiful turtle-shaped graves. About twenty-five percent of the Indigenous population lost their lives.

Prior to the twentieth century, Okinawa was the main island of the Ryukyu Kingdom and traded peacefully with China and Japan. In the sinister manner of colonialism, once Japan gained control of the islands, the languages and culture of the Indigenous people were severely restricted or forbidden. When sugar cane was introduced to the islands, the Indigenous people were indentured as slave labour. There are many similarities to my own country of Australia, the direct result of the greed that defined colonialism.

When I lived on Okinawa, the war in Vietnam was still going, and the American military had all of its bases there. In fact, after the end of World War Two, the island was annexed from Japan to the United States. Most Americans didn't engage with the locals and did their shopping on their PX or BX exchanges, stores that sold everything they would buy in America, from mattresses to meat.

All bases were gated, so one had to show papers to get in. We had stickers on our windscreens, personal identity papers and military number plates. Schools, hospitals, and everything else were inside the bases. The island teemed with the various defence forces, marine, army, and air force personnel were everywhere throughout the island. Certain streets had signs saying that only Okinawans could go past that point. Some people told me those areas were for gambling and gangland activity.

Special Forces families were grouped in designated housing. There was a hierarchy about which I knew nothing. Growing up in Australia, especially regional Australia, the only war artefact of any description was the memorial where we held an ANZAC service every April.

Richard, a captain, had five other men in his elite, clandestine team. All these men were highly strung and deadly silent killers, so hypervigilant that they would leap under the table when a champagne cork popped. The military kept them separate from the regular soldiers, both in housing and at social clubs.

As the captain's wife, I was expected to guide and look after the wives while the "A" team was about their orders. That didn't happen, because I had come from a place where we knew nothing about military life. Besides, it didn't seem to matter to Richard, who was proud of me despite my woefulness as an officer's wife. I was the only Australian on base and suspect I was excused for the many social mistakes I made at parades and formal balls.

There was so much formality! Parades were important, and one was expected to attend. There were even designated places where wives were supposed to sit. Medal ceremonies and very formal balls, where long white gloves were worn by the women, were common. Even the soldiers wore gloves as we danced. Everyone was kind to me, and any of my foibles were put down to my *Aussie-ness*. Coming from a democratic place, I had no idea it was considered impolite to wander up and say hello to a general or colonel, all of whom were extremely polite and interested in asking me about Australia.

I wandered the boondocks for most of my time there and got to know the Okinawan people, who, for some reason, thought I was

French. Okinawans hated being considered Japanese and discreetly sneered at the size, noise, and greed of the occupying American forces. They refused to converse in Japanese and made me teach them English. I grew to love these stocky, honest, and intelligent people.

Narrow streets wound through high-walled villages. The walls of houses were made of great cubes of coral. At low tide, you could walk along the coral beaches and see how the blocks had been cut from the ancient reefs. I spent many sunny days squatting in some leafy street with my watercolours and paper, trying to capture fleeting images of the beauty of their tessellated roofs and gorgeous dry coral walls.

The boys were enrolled in preschool, and I spent my days snorkelling over beautiful reefs in waters that only had waves when there was a typhoon. I loved street food, was happy walking past a smelly benjo ditch, and learnt how to scuba dive. You had to be careful where you walked, as the benjo ditches were open sewers.

Today has been a rare day of blue, cloudless skies. Just before the sun sets, I'm taking my dogs for a sniff and a wander. The soft pinks and pastels of this winter sky reflect their colours onto the wet sand. This sand is familiar to the soles of my feet, so different from the pure white sand of Okuma Beach at the northern tip of Okinawa, where we were stationed in the seventies.

This was an exclusive retreat for the US military. Richard was out of the country on another Temporary Duty. He didn't know the extent of this duty but told me that officer personnel could stay for free at this five-star resort, so I decided to give the boys a treat.

Unfortunately, I suffered a migraine headache after our drive north, so once I had registered us at the administration building and we were given keys to our beachfront cottage, I lay down with a wet towel over my forehead. I trusted my boys completely but was certainly a risk-taking mother.

## Next Foot Forward

I woke when two Okinawan gardeners knocked on the door to advise me, in broken English, that I had lost a son. Both boys had gone to do archery at the supervised activities ground. Simon had grabbed the bow and arrow and hit a bullseye. Damian, always earnest, ran down to pull the arrow out. As he did, a dog jumped up to play with him. When Damian put his hand up to stop the dog from biting his face, he inadvertently stuck the arrow deep into his own head.

"I came to consciousness in a shed, Mother. Two old men had pliers and were trying to get the arrowhead out. I was bleeding everywhere on my face."

Damian, like me, hated being touched without warning, so he simply got up and ran away, heading off down the road to wherever he thought home was. By that time, the military police had been called, and there was a general hunt for a little four-year-old with a shock of bright silver hair.

Damian has an inbuilt GPS system. On land or sea, I've never known him to be lost. Even in a city, he can somehow find his inner coordinates and achieve his desired direction. I envy him that.

The police found him jogging along a dirt track deep inside a sugarcane farm, heading straight for Australia. I was an immensely proud mother and rejected the offer of stitches, as I knew he would not tolerate any further interference with his body.

# Chapter 22

In 1972, the Okinawans held fiery demonstrations because the USA was handing them back to Japan. Ethnic Okinawans were not Japanese and, from what I could understand, were of Mongolian or Chinese descent. They had been used as slaves by the Japanese prior to World War II, and in the southern end of the island is a place called Suicide Cliff, where thousands leapt to their deaths because they were told by their masters, the Japanese, that American troops would kill them so horribly their spirits would be doomed to roam forever. They tried to demonstrate for independence but were instead returned to Japan.

As I think back, once again I had not placed myself in a position to make friends because I spent most of my life outside the military complexes. The noise and camaraderie of the military wives, their ignorance of world events, and their true paranoia about all things Chinese and Russian bored me to death. I am constitutionally unable to gossip, had no common interests with the women I met, and was perhaps a little snobby in my Australian-ness.

Communication with the locals consisted of facial expressions, hand gestures, and the occasional word here and there. Okinawans had round faces, seemingly always smiling. They nodded even while we were trying to understand each other. Life with Richard was easy. He was forever leaving in the dead of night or coming home strained and weary. We were blessed to be able to accept each other. I think he was proud of his family and was lovely with the boys.

### Next Foot Forward

# Chapter 23

It is early winter here now, on the east coast of NSW, and time to fish for tailor, a time of cold westerly winds, chilly mornings and evenings, and long casting rods. While we have a choice, I prefer fishing from the beach, using either a shining silver seventy-gram lure or pilchards threaded on a ganged hook.

Let me tell you about fishing for this wonderful, fighting, and delicious creature. We walk up the steep gravel track, listening to the birds as they flit through the tuckeroo trees and monkey vines. The dust on this track is always warm as we head over to Back Beach, a favourite fishing spot. Please allow me to put you in this experience.

The wind and seas are calming down after a five-day rage. Turmoil is everywhere, and this shoreline, which I love like a poem, memorised, is a discourteous place. The air crackles statically on my hair and skin. I could be on a faraway planet. It smells of Cambrian times. Seabirds wheel high like tiny fighter jets, minuscule SR-71s, then flay themselves through the sea's skin. The booming swell comes and goes as I stand in a lost memory, echoes of a low incendiary growl.

While I rig my twelve-foot big rod with the three-ounce spinner, the atmospheric frenzy relays itself to the baitfish. Whitebait. I call them glitterfish, for they remind me of spilt sequins as they flirt through the waves. They are coiling and roiling outside the break, in an organic and measured ballet. They are being hunted by my target fish: tailor, a streamlined predator, a pelagic super-fighter.

This fancy spinner will be irresistible to them, with its fluorescent clarity and glamorous shaping, as it flicks through the glitterfish. I notice that the sand is cold, sending pain up through my shins. Better that I am knee-deep and numb for this action. I ponder the peculiarity of my relationship with creatures of the sea. I am familiar with the deadly, the strange, the beautiful, and now, the edible. The grey nurse sharks that swim with me; the beautiful cowrie and murex shells I collect; the seagrass beds that dance in the currents and provide shelter for baby fish, and now, my dinner.

As I cast my line and crank my long rod, the wattles and tallowwoods pump out their final blossoms and pollens in the heathland behind me. Wattlebirds clack in the dying light and the willy wagtail claims ownership of this place, or did he accompany me?

Alone here, I am charged to the eyelids. Time comes and goes in waves and pleats, like the water I stand in. Perhaps time is moving through me, not I through time. Again and again, the rod tip bends, the top third of the stick arching impossibly as I reel in and set the drag. They fight in streamlined glory and are dispatched and bled before their silver and blue dull. I ache with happiness as the wind rakes through my hair and thrums its atavistic rhythm along my taut line. Then... they are gone. I have my bag limit.

I stand exhausted, hands swollen, knuckles tight with salted skin and blood-rimmed nails. It is night. Now, I am a feather riding light. How I would have loved to share this experience with Richard, who is, like me, growing old far away in a different country.

Next Foot Forward

# Chapter 24

After one of Richard's TDYs, he arrived back more stressed and withdrawn than usual.

"Not a good trip?" I asked.

He opened a beer, took a long drink that ended in a weary sigh. "Nothing went to plan, babe. Don't ask. We were out of country. Turned into a shit show. Let's go have dinner at the club."

I knew there was nothing more to be said. We packed the boys into the jeep and asked the mamasan to finish the laundry and feed Samson, our dog.

Dinner was fine. We joined the other members of his A Team and chatted about nothing important. We wives had learnt to carry the conversation by gossiping about the letters we received from our families and the goings-on in our respective countries. The American women were fascinated to hear about our spiders, venomous reptiles, and sharks. They thought the scars on my legs were the result of a great white shark attack, and I never did tell them the truth.

During the next three days that Richard was home, he was obviously avoiding both boys. Where he used to read to them before they went to sleep, excuses were made. He had to check his parachute jump records or read up on his next orders. Instead of dropping them off at kindergarten on his way to headquarters, he arranged for them to go on the base bus.

One day, Simon came home from kindy pale and having trouble breathing. His pulse was very slow, which was a warning sign for me.

I found my husband polishing his boots in our mudroom.

"I need to get Simon to the base doctors, Richard."

"It's down near Naha. You'll just need my social security number, Lina. I'll be gone by the time you get back. We're moving out to another in-country tonight. Good luck!"

After a forty-minute drive south, we were seen by the only paediatrician on the island. The base hospital was just a long Quonset hut, with a central aisle and rooms down each side. There weren't any advanced care facilities available for children, mostly just a setup for colds and vaccinations. I suspected that most mothers of chronically ill children chose to stay stateside.

During the following week, we had five trips to the base medics, who wanted all of Simon's files. That was quite a drama. I had to phone my brother in Sydney, who managed to get Simon's entire medical history from the Children's Hospital. It was rushed to Richmond Airfield, where an American Air Force plane was waiting to get them over to Okinawa. When the medic saw the enormous file and the surgeries Simon had already been through, he contacted Richard's boss and told him that I would have to take my son over to Letterman Medical Centre as soon as possible. I received orders to get Simon to the US.

Richard was still out of country, so I arranged for Damian to be cared for by the Colonel's wife.

"Go, Lina. I will enjoy having this little man for a week or so. Worry about nothing," was the advice of this very sweet lady, who was never seen without an elegant beehive hairdo and bright vermilion lipstick as she hosted tea afternoons for the wives.

Next Foot Forward

# Chapter 25

I am scared of planes. Always have been, ever since my parents hired a light plane to take me over the Great Dividing Range, back to my first school placement after my degree, probably in 1964. The Cessna crashed in a paddock near Inverell, in the northern tablelands of New South Wales.

I came to consciousness with a seat on top of me, and the pilot, whose name was Harvey, was nonchalantly untangling bits and pieces while I crawled out. He flagged down a motorist to take me the rest of the way and assured me he hadn't sustained serious damage. I often wonder if my father got his money back, because you couldn't say I was safely delivered!

We travelled lightly, because I had learnt there was no one to help you carry baggage on military airfields. With Simon's pyjamas, a chess set, and three pairs of T-shirts and undies, I boarded the medivac plane with my heart in my mouth and a kind of desperation. Life always got ahead of my brain, my body, and my train of thought. There never seemed to be a choice for me.

I was in an aeroplane, a C-131, to be exact, strapped into a long, hollow bullet casing. A claustrophobic experience. My seat faced the tail end, and these military planes do not take off like a regular jet. To save fuel, they go straight up. At perpendicular, I was facing a massive drop, many metres down to the tail. There was no décor. Everything was grey. Racks of dull green and occupied body bags were strapped to the wall across the aisle.

My five-year-old son, who had a congenital heart problem, and I had boarded at Kadena Air Force Base to visit a specialist in California. Because of a typhoon, we were diverted to the Philippines. There, a cohort of drug-addicted soldiers was brought on and seated down the tail end, on the same side as the dead bodies. I assumed those poor boys were going back to America for rehabilitation. Everything about war is ugly.

## Adelina Basile

Stormy weather bucketed us.

*"Hitting a bit of weather here, guys. We'll go south around Guam,"* said the pilot through the loudspeaker.

Boys coming home from 'Nam came drugged, or in body bags stacked tightly on top of each other. The war was officially over, but there were still a lot of sons, brothers, and fathers to bring home. Some were dead; many were addicted. They were sent home on these medivac flights.

During the time we spent in Okinawa, Japan, my eldest son, Simon, had increasingly alarming heart episodes. The U.S. military decided that we would be better served by being sent to the military hospital, the Letterman Medical Hospital, which was situated in the beautiful Presidio of San Francisco.

This was a hauntingly picturesque place, where the mists came wafting in across the bay and hung low and dense, making visibility impossible. Through those grey swirls came the eerie calls of foghorns. They resembled the call of the powerful owl I recalled from my early childhood.

Simon and a cardiac paediatrician occupied the seats in front of me during this flight. Beyond them was an assortment of ailing people, a woman in labour, her screams bouncing around the walls of the plane like echoes in a cave; and a man on a stretcher in front of Simon, who was suddenly being bagged for anaesthetic by an army nurse.

There were no privacy screens, and it was clearly an emergency, because he was cut open right in front of us. The plane was anything but stable, and the nurse kept wobbling past me down the aisle carrying bags of blood, and, I suspect, some excised part of the poor man. Behind me was the bulkhead and the crew and pilot space.

## Next Foot Forward

*"Hold on, ladies and gentlemen. Shit! We've caught the edge of that fucking typhoon. This could be uncomfortable!"* said the captain, who never turned the loudspeaker off.

A bit later, he yelled, *"We could pull some Gs!"*, military talk.

The plane dropped and banked sharply, and before I knew it, the body bags had rocked themselves loose and were rolling and spilling across the aisle and onto my legs. You could picture a horror movie in which an army of giant caterpillars had decided to start a riot. They were heavy, cumbersome, and rolling about totally out of control, some landing and clogging the aisle beside my seat.

In front of me, Simon was being given oxygen, and further down, the doctors and nurses were trying to keep their balance while stopping the man from sliding off his operating stretcher.

I tried to get out of my seat to help and felt desperately ashamed as I stumbled and fell into the pile. No one could help because most of the staff and crew were attending to the person on the operating table, that unfortunate but unconscious man right out in the open in front of us.

Jerking and galloping like an angry horse, this warhorse of an aeroplane had a mind of its own and rodeoed through the worst of the typhoon. Glancing across the aisle into the tail section, I watched another nurse hurriedly injecting those medicated soldiers, who had started to become angry and unruly as they tried to undo their safety belts and find some freedom. Truly, it was a scene from hell.

Despite all my inner meditations, I had come totally unstuck with panic.

*"Keep it together, Lina. Big breaths! I can do this for Simon!"*

Closing my eyes, I took myself back to that little beach in Australia, the one where I was safe, and did my breathing exercises to imaginary breaking waves. I pictured the rocks reflecting themselves in clear water as they gave homes to the little crabs and listened to the gentle sough of the waves breaking exhaustedly on the low tide.

The scent of drying sea grasses and kelp grew strong in my mind, and for a while, I was filled with an inchoate longing and sadness for my childhood home. Without thinking, I hung onto the arm of the man seated to my left. He was a tall, good-looking African American in a marine uniform and wordless. He endured my clutching until we landed at Hickam Air Force Base in Hawaii.

Sitting almost immobile the whole way, he reminded me of a carved totem pole I had seen in books about the Canadian Inuit people. My breath exhaled like that of a trumpeter with a passion for cigarettes. Panic had changed my breathing.

As we taxied to a stop, the air was split by sirens as police and ambulances tore across the tarmac towards us. The captain asked us all to stay in our seats until further notice.

The doors were opened, and four military police marched into the plane, straight down the aisle toward me, high-stepping over the body bags that hadn't yet been strapped back down. I was nodded to the side, and they handcuffed the marine beside me, the man who had been my strength for six hours. He was marched out ahead of all the hospital cases on board.

That man had been the Norfolk pine tree of my childhood, the gnarly-barked guardian whose sap wept a tangy gum I would eat while I read beneath its sheltering shade. Here I was, half a world from the only place I'd never wanted to leave. Life had sidestepped me into another alien scenario. With no real options, it was always just one step forward for me.

When we were allowed to stretch our legs during refuelling, I found out that the marine had totally lost his mind back in Vietnam and had killed three of his platoon in their mess hall in Saigon, now called Ho Chi Minh City.

A psychiatrist once told me that torturers never need to use any tool of torture if they can cause a true panic attack in a person. Just remembering that medivac flight makes my hair prickle, and I can feel the tension and fear building inside my heart and head.

My nana used to say, *"War turns a man rancid,"* as she thought aloud about what she called *"The Troubles."* Her uncles and cousins were Irish Republicans. That phrase had stuck in my head, but for the first time, I understood it, in context.

A military hospital is very orderly. They were ready for Simon and, after receiving his files, put him through many tests and consultations. It wasn't until one specialist turned to me, smiling, and said, *"We feel privileged to have had the opportunity to observe your son's heart,"* that I realised again how easy it had been to forget what his heart had already suffered.

Finally, a child psychologist was called in to talk with Simon, and the diagnosis was that of *"emotional and psychological aetiology"* which was somehow affecting his heart rhythms. They suggested that, sometime in the future, he would need a pacemaker and some more complicated surgery, but for the present, they wanted us to manage the situation by seeking some family counselling.

It should be remembered that his heart was very experimental, and is, to this day.

We were booked to cross back over to Okinawa on another military aircraft via Alaska. During the time he was in hospital, I had fallen down some stairs in the visitors' quarters and had damaged some ribs, so it was a painful flight for me with my bandaged ribs. It was also a painful trip for the Air Force pilot who sat next to me. He was so nervous at take-off that I could hardly believe he was an active pilot. He was counting altimeters in his head and muttering numbers, and when we hit some C.A.T. (which

I learnt was clear air turbulence), he almost hid on the floor of the plane as it dropped our stomachs.

Richard was again out of the country, but I had been informed that the General's wife had been notified of our return date. It was Halloween evening, and no one was waiting to meet us at Naha International Airport. Party time on the base! We taxied from Naha to our officers' quarters and found that my mother was hosting a party and had claimed Damian from the General.

This woman! Such a force! Somehow, reader, it is beyond my ken to understand her powers, she had flown up, landed as an Australian civilian at an Okinawan international airport, and ferociously demanded to be taken to the quarters of the occupying commanding officer. And so, she was. It seems that she then decided to have a Halloween party, as it was an American thing to do, and promptly forgot that no one would meet us as we flew in from the USA.

*"Thank heavens you're back,"* I sighed as I hugged Richard. *"Mother's here!"*

Each time he returned from duty, my heart cracked at the weariness and pain that pushed the bones of his face into sharp silhouette. His dedication to duty, in such an impossible war, held me in a confused awe. I felt that my mother was showing concern for her grandchildren by flying such a distance; however, she had terrible timing. Richard obviously needed downtime, and I was anxious for Mother to be gone.

After I saw her off, we resumed our loving and considered intimacy. My husband was unable to sleep and broke into a boiling sweat that drenched our sheets in the night. I gently tried to discover his state of mind without stressing him further. He finally revealed that one of his missions had gone badly wrong, and some children had been killed. He felt that he couldn't look at the boys.

## Next Foot Forward

It had been suggested by the specialists over in San Francisco that we seek some family counselling, which I was keen to do, as I felt it could be something we could easily fix.

When Richard read the report from the cardiologist, his whole body seemed to shatter and melt like an icy pole in the sun, this man I loved so totally.

*"Lina, I can't do this."*

I heard his words and saw the torment on his face. It hit me quite suddenly that I would have to choose between Simon's health or my love for Richard.

*"Are you talking about the counselling, sweetheart?"*

He put both arms around me and leant his forehead against mine. *"I can't have a psychological note on my record. I'll lose my clearance."*

He explained to me that if he did that, he would no longer be able to do the job he loved so much. I thought he was exaggerating. We shared no anger or ill feelings and continued to try to work out what to do. For me. For my children. For him, my idealistic, romantic lover, and for his country.

*"Are you sure? What do other people do? Let's go see Colonel Gerassi. There might be a way around it."*

We made an appointment and went to headquarters. The Colonel had a soft spot for me and was a great dancer, often partnering me at official balls while Richard was out of the country.

*"It's true, Lina. Rules are rules in this man's army. You guys will have to decide for yourselves."*

My husband of only eighteen months was telling me the truth. It would end the career that was his life. This was a man who had survived forty-nine consecutive months in the most secret parts of

## Adelina Basile

Laos and Cambodia during the Vietnam War. I knew it would destroy him to give up the military, and I knew there was never a better companion for me in this entire world.

Clinging to each other, we agreed to divorce, which was simple in Shinto land and required only a trip to a Japanese post office. Because he was always on call, we finalised all the military paperwork, which left me as an illegal alien in Japan, within a week. He had again flown away to jump from a plane into danger, somewhere as perilous as North Korea.

My mind sparked like a live wire in a storm. Once more, I was faced with uncertainty, despair, and a frightening sense of doom. Generously, he told me to take anything the boys and I needed, as we would have to live outside the base.

It never crossed my mind to go back to Australia. I had no money anyway, as we had lived on his pay cheque.

A few days later, as I was trying to sort my life out, driving from the base to collect my children, I was suddenly seized by a fear so vast it stripped the world away. Thought vanished. The road dissolved. Air itself disappeared, as if the universe had folded inward and left me suspended in a void.

I slammed the brakes, convinced that I was dying, not gradually, but immediately, absolutely. I couldn't breathe, not in the panicked sense of gasping, but as if oxygen no longer existed. My chest locked. The space around me pressed in, silent and suffocating. I broke into a clammy sweat and slumped forward, forehead pressed to the wheel, unable to call for help, unable to move.

Time didn't stretch, it disappeared, and I lay inside that black moment, unreachable.

Finally coming to consciousness, I told myself I was just too stressed by my situation. However, for the next thirty years of my

## Next Foot Forward

life, there were times when I had to endure this horrible incapacity, called a *panic attack*, which left me always guilty and fearful of the next one.

## Chapter 26

During my SCUBA diving course, I became acquainted with an airman from Arizona. He worked as an assistant to the instructor, and I often bumped into him at the reef while scavenging for shells. When I explained my situation to him, he mentioned that the house the instructor lived in off-base was empty, as the man had been sent to Thailand on temporary duty. They were both Air Force specialists, and he agreed to try to contact the instructor, Clark, to see if I could move in.

Which we did.

It was a difficult time, as the boys couldn't go to school, and I couldn't buy petrol on base because I had handed all my documents back to Richard. The little house was nestled in the boondocks, surrounded by other Okinawan fishermen's homes. A Chinese lady who lived nearby was always offering food to the boys.

Clark, my dive instructor, had made it very clear during my SCUBA classes that when he finished his time in the Air Force, he was heading for the Great Barrier Reef in Australia. Between lectures, we had spent many hours talking about Australia and its coastlines. He intended to start a charter boat for dive excursions.

About the fifth Saturday after the boys and I had been living there, three Okinawan policemen drove up. Despite our very limited communication, they made it clear that I was to be arrested and taken to the police station. I told the boys to go over to the Chinese lady and went with the police. "Richard, where are you?" I thought. Looking back, everything in my life seems so random, so erratic, and not quite sane.

There was no embassy or consulate on Okinawa. Often my letters home went via Austria. I was put in a room while the policemen rounded up an interpreter. I still don't understand how they knew

## Next Foot Forward

so quickly that I was no longer under the auspices of the US Military. As a dependant, I didn't have a visa. That was now a problem, as it seemed Richard should have given me a little brown book that I could have taken to a post office to be stamped once a month. Neither of us knew that, and besides, he never knew from one minute to the next where he was being dropped in. For all I knew, he had probably already left the island.

I convinced the police that I would go up to Tokyo, promising the boys as collateral. After they drove me home, I organised a plane ticket and, using hand signals, asked the Chinese neighbour to look after the boys. I really was so brave in emergencies! It was years before I learned that I was a PTSD sufferer, and autistic as well. Strangely enough, in real emergencies, my panic never attacks me. It's a sneaky illness that comes like a cloak of blackness when I'm going quite well in the sea of life.

I sat on my bed packing my knapsack, trying to remain calm and determined. I took myself off into my mind, back to the sweet-scented air of Australia, to the secluded beach of my childhood, while the taxi was on its way. I wanted to run on the beach with my dog; to throw myself, however clothed, into the rock pool and gaze at the azure above; to catch my breath in delight at the underbelly of the osprey and sea eagle; to sit on the dune and hold my breath as the glitterfish jumped and swarmed in the surf break; to poke my fingers and toes into the soft, sensuous guts of the tunicates and turn over the urchins so they could make their way back to safety. To cover myself in sand, roll down the dune into the sea, and just be safe.

# Chapter 27

The Australian Embassy in Tokyo was easy to find, and it was such a relief to be speaking my own language. I was shown into a large room where a man sat behind quite an impressive desk. In front of him was a stack of papers in a file.

"I'm Lina Basile," I said.

He laughed and slapped the papers with his hand. "Yes, you are. And at this moment, you are our most embarrassing citizen!" He tapped the papers, grinning. "This pile of papers is our file on you!"

How relieved I was that I was Australian!

Then he asked if I would like a Devonshire tea and phoned out an order. Soon we were chatting over scones with cream and tea, and I was telling him what had happened so far in my life. Thinking back, those bureaucrats probably already knew what had gone wrong anyway.

When I finished, I asked him what would happen next. I was horrified to hear that the boys and I would be deported back to Australia. When I asked if that was a free trip, I found out that it was not. I told him my mother would kill me because of the shame. For all I knew, they were probably used to stories like mine.

He said there was another option, to find another military man to marry me. He asked if I knew of anyone. I thought of the man whose house I was living in and knew he wanted to live on the reef in Queensland when he retired from the Air Force. I took a punt and said yes.

How I loved this embassy man! He took the photos from the boys' and my passports, and while I spent a few hours chatting with him, magic happened.

## Next Foot Forward

About two hours later, three individual passports were presented to me, all with false surnames but with our photos. By the time I left the embassy, the whole staff was wishing me luck. I had to get back to Okinawa, contact Clark, and get married at another post office. (I still have those precious passports.)

While I was away, my friend from Arizona had contacted Clark, and the day after I returned to the little green house in the boondocks, he turned up. We made our own contract, I would get protection, and he would gain Aussie citizenship. He had four more years to complete in the Air Force and was happy to make this deal, as he knew it would be difficult to become a resident of Australia without a good reason. A marriage would make it easy. He had already researched it long before he even met me.

His job was different from Richard's, and life became very stable. The boys could enrol back into the base schools, and I was free to drive wherever I wanted on the many bases across the island. His expertise was marine science, and the island was perfect for us all, as we loved the ocean and its creatures.

Clark had been diving all around the world and was intent on building a scientific shell collection. He traded or bought shells whenever he discovered specific species for sale. He was a member of a mollusc collection society and intended to write a comprehensive scientific shell manual when he retired.

He never encroached on my privacy or my life. We developed a mutual respect, and once he was granted base quarters and had moved, I took a teaching position at Christ the King Mission School. It was run by an American Catholic missionary order and was necessary because half-caste children were not permitted in the state schools on Okinawa.

It was outside the bases and filled with children of every colour and hue. As the American base schools did not impress me, I transferred the boys to this school, where I felt they would learn more discipline. They even had to wear a uniform. This involved a great deal of extra work for me, but I could envision only satisfactory results from this new venture. As de Chardin would have said, "Limits to my ability did not exist."

Once we were safe, my panic attacks became more frequent. It seemed that I needed an existential crisis to function. Due to Clark's total lack of responsibility, we were frequently put to the test of survival.

He owned a Zodiac, an inflatable with a powerful outboard engine, made famous by Jacques Cousteau. As Clark was a collector of molluscs, we spent every spare minute out on the water. Sometimes it was quite unnerving being anchored out in the middle of the China Sea with no land in sight. The boys and I fished from the boat while Clark threw himself overboard with a tank on his back in search of an elusive mollusc.

I wasn't strong enough to pull the engine start rope, and we often waited for close to an hour while the wind came up and the boat pulled hard against its anchor. I spent those times making up stories for the boys or letting them snorkel as close as possible to the boat. It was too deep for free diving.

This was not my generous and soothing ocean, but one that people scoured for black coral and rare shells.

It was the last weekend before the school term began, and the boys were wild with freedom. We had taken the Zodiac to a deserted island, our packs stuffed with dive gear and cameras, but not a scrap of food. These trips were my "survival tests." We knew how to fish, dive, and spear. Simon was our snarer, building elaborate traps from nothing but sticks and grasses.

I watched as the boys raced around the island, their skinny, spindly brown legs pumping like pistons.

"Look, Mother! I found a spring. Fresh water!" Damian grinned with satisfaction. That child could thrive anywhere. His curiosity

## Next Foot Forward

was endless. If he phoned me today, he'd likely offer a detailed lecture on the ants' behaviour and why it would rain in exactly two and a half days.

The island was lush with possibility.

"Simon, that's not a coconut, it's a sea mine," Clark joked, squinting at a rusted orb near the tideline.

Simon scoffed. "Still might float."

Soon we had a rabbit and two flounder roasting over beach stones, Simon's snares had worked, and my hunting had filled the gaps. The sun was beginning to tilt low when Damian paused mid-dig.

"Mother... does the sky usually look like that?"

I turned. An unnatural green cloud lumbered up from the southeast, heavy and ominous. The air had changed, metallic, thick. I could smell the wind shifting.

"Come on, Clark. Time to pack up."

Once outside the cove, we were hit by three-metre swells and vicious surf chop. Okinawan timber boats were splintering in the distance, breaking apart in the chaos. The rain was horizontal, pelting and bruising us. Each gust of wind slapped the Zodiac like an angry hand. Nature was in full fury, raw, relentless.

Samson stood proudly at the prow, tongue lolling in a joyful, defiant grin, barking into the storm as if it were his sparring partner. Damian had curled into a ball under the bow, sucking his thumb. Simon sat straight beside me while I murmured Hail Marys aloud. Clark kept steady hands on the tiller.

We navigated blindly, riding the swell with equal parts guesswork and desperate instinct. Had we not been weighed down by scuba tanks, cameras, and camping gear, I'm sure we would've capsized.

## Adelina Basile

We finally made landfall at White Beach, the U.S. naval facility, eerie beneath a sickly green sky that cast an otherworldly glow over the dock. Alarms shrieked overhead; the island was on lockdown. The typhoon had arrived.

Salt hung in the air like grit. Okinawan homes were built to collapse under pressure; concrete military housing would fare better. As we dragged ourselves up the ramp, drenched and trembling, we were intercepted by military police.

"You folks need to be indoors," one shouted, eyes wide at the sight of our bedraggled crew. "You came in that?"

Clark nodded. "We rode the storm like surfers. They're Aussies," he said, indicating the three of us, bedraggled and soaked. "Almost didn't make it."

The officer shook his head, waving us through. "Get in before she takes another swing."

**Next Foot Forward**

# Chapter 28

These days, I have a bit of a laugh when I hear on the radio an urgent notice that a category two cyclone is soon to cross our coast. "Alfred" did that just a few months back. We have so much warning of weather events now that I can never understand why people aren't prepared all the time for the various stages of our weather cycle. Since the last bushfires, I've kept a bag packed on my verandah with everything I need to escape in a hurry.

The climate has been interfered with by our human activities, mostly fossil fuel burning and deforestation. The latter is a form of genocide against a variety of species.

I have great affection for a living tree. It hums when I hug it. Its sturdiness bestows solace, and I can read stories in the shapes and textures of its bark. Its resilience and growth leave me in awe. A myriad of fauna call the tree home, and we are brothers and sisters on this planet together. Lying now in the shade of my fully leafed jacaranda, I am aware that my planet will never be defeated. It is my species that has been earmarked for extinction.

Okinawa at that time had no industry except fishing and sugar cane growing. The air was pure, and as both boys had a tendency to play with the indigenous children rather than the American ones, they were free to roam and explore to their hearts' content. We adopted the Japanese diet and tried, but failed, to learn the language. The Okinawans were desperate to speak English. If you denied them that, they lost face, so most conversations were held in broken English, hand and face signals, with a little bit of French thrown in.

Let me tell you what a terrible mother I am. One day, while Clark was on temporary duty in another country, the boys and I visited one of our native friends. He sometimes dived with us. His wife, Mrs Nakamura, gestured for us to come into the house. This was an enormous privilege, as mostly Okinawans took you out to a restaurant rather than inviting you into their homes.

It was a sunny day. She was in her small alcove kitchen, a pair of cooking chopsticks in her hand, bent over her fryer. The most wonderfully enticing aroma filled the air, and I nodded, sniffed, and clapped my hands to indicate my appreciation. She withdrew a piece of shiny white flesh and held it up just as I was asking what fish it was. She placed it into my open mouth, and as it was going down my throat, she murmured, "Fuffa." Before it had reached my stomach, I had translated it to "Puffer." (Okinawans could not pronounce the "P" sound.)

Everyone in Japan is, or was, warned that the pufferfish is deadly toxic, and at that time there were only three chefs on the island licensed to prepare it. This is what went through my head:

"I am going to die."

"There is no Australian embassy here."

"My family doesn't know where I'm living on this island."

"The boys and I will all have to die together because they'll be traumatised if I abandon them like this."

So, as I thought I was halfway dead, I pulled the boys over and said with a smile, "Yummy," and "Taste this." Mrs Nakamura, with a very pleased expression, fed a piece to each of the boys.

We didn't die, but to this day I feel the shame of my instinct on that day. Sometimes I can rationalise it and decide that there had been so much trauma in my life until then, and I was still only thirty-two years old, I had not yet reached some capacity for sense.

# Chapter 29

There are still no people in my story. It worries me greatly that I have been unable to join interest groups and mix socially. I believe this was one of the reasons I so frustrated my very social mother. My analyst tells me not to worry about this, as I always have multiple dogs at my side, and I finally understand that the trees, wind, ocean, and all the fauna I have learnt to love, rescue, rehabilitate and release, serve the same purpose as friends.

It took me many years to find a psychologist or social worker who could read between my lines and recognise me as a person desperate for help. Half of my life was spent worrying that I would never be mentally healthy because there was so much emphasis on "being social" in the health guidelines of the day. Well, I am healthy, but my friends are not humans.

I sound awkward, even to myself.

Rockpools are scattered among the volcanic rock ledges below my headland. I know their inhabitants and have profound respect for the tiny ecosystems within.

I have named a favourite sea urchin Thorndyke, and today I squat to observe his neighbourhood. This is what unfolded. It is sad but inevitable, like my life.

Thorndyke the sea urchin was restless. The tide was fully out, and he tried to settle himself comfortably between the sand and coral while he pondered the advisability of eating now or later.

His pool was still and clear, the rapid darting of the damselfish family making intermittent ripples across the surface. Ogdin (the name I give his neighbour), his bivalve pectin friend, was awake, his eyes twinkling and sparkling like tiny jewel drops in the shimmering water. The sun sent sharp shafts of pure light streaking into the pool, and Thorndyke watched amusedly as the minnows played, jumping over and ducking under the beams.

The anemones were also awake. Aware of their beauty, they performed a symphony of dance, their arms reaching, swaying, and beckoning, shamelessly beautiful in the clear silence of the pool.

Thorndyke felt old. He had watched the baby damsel since she was born, before, when the waters were warmer. They had come rushing north, currents of warmth carrying the numerous and myriad forms of new life, depositing them like gifts in a flourish of swirls, curtseys, and intricate eddies, safely into his pool.

He sighed. It seemed so long ago. As he pondered the past, he could feel his topmost spines grow warm. They were halfway out of the water, and the new sensation of air, touching and gentle, felt good. He allowed himself the luxury of a stretch, then suddenly caught a glimpse of a shadow across the bottom of the pool. Thorndyke froze. He dared not move; his spines pushed out stiff and firm, drawing him closer to the coral overhang. He sensed his enemy, the newest addition to the tidal pool community.

The blue-green crab slunk from behind the coral, his stalked eyes missing nothing. Empty, colourless eyes.

Mother Damsel swooped down and nipped at the crab's antennae, a harsh, brave warning to stay away from her family.

The crab now stood high, legs up, giant strides taking him sideways, closer to Thorndyke. The sea urchin tried to draw himself further into the sand, a gnawing emptiness in his gut. Two big claws gripped him mercilessly. His spines crushed under the claws, and he looked towards Ogdin for help. With a swift jet of water, Ogdin closed his door.

## Next Foot Forward

The crab gave a tremendous heave, and Thorndyke was rolled over, his opening exposed, his strong beak of a mouth no match against the tearing claws...

...and the pain. The unbearable pulling pain as part of his tender body was wrenched from his fragile shell. Then he felt nothing.

The damsel family were having their siesta, resting suspended in the holes and cracks of the coral. The female, lazily twitching sideways, caught a subtle aroma of something delicious. She finned hastily, greedily, in its direction and was soon lunching delightedly on the tiny morsels of white flesh that floated up through the arms of the crab. The sea urchin had completed his circuit of life in his tide pool.

Oftentimes I feel akin to that sea urchin. There is always someone or something bigger, louder, angrier in my life with people. I think I have grown spines of my own.

If you took that step and visited me, we could share the somebody-ness of us as we sit speckled by the sun while it fights its way through the leaves of my lemon myrtle tree. If you visited me, when you visit me, we would find the common sense of goodness in this time of modernity. We would discover that we live in so many persistently unmodern things... dreams, illness, memory... and, what is love? There is nothing modern about a kangaroo or a grey shrike-thrush. These unmodern ones are my people. We are each other and cannot exist separately.

As I sat in our little one-mast dinghy yesterday, fishing for a bream, I drafted a poem in my head, and now I will write it for you. You may notice that I look down upon myself from on high, I always have, and my paintings reflect the same perspective.

### The Fisher-girl

And words will fail a girl, staring about in this empty grey.

## Adelina Basile

Straining eyes against the frosting fog which lies

Thicker than a shroud about a vault.

(How insignificant one can seem.)

No separation exists here between the heaven and the hell.

A lonely craft and its occupant,

Suspended in a monotone, like a spider in its web.

Friendly, creaking wood.

The stark realism of a tiny spire

Standing like a shot against the empty mist, her company.

She is alone. Her sun now hidden,

Lost somewhere in that rich and tasteless fog.

And her Earth?

Is it a million miles away?

Or does it lie ahead,

Perhaps to wound her tiny craft and leave her

Struck with fears of dying?

Where are the gulls?

Where is her home?

And the sea is so still…

And the fisher-girl does not.

Oh, you dreaded day, you monster!

Do you come to petrify a soul?

## Next Foot Forward

If so, go away, your job is done…

But it does not.

And the sea is lonelier still.

## Chapter 30

They tell me you cannot remember being born or, indeed, the first few years of your life. There are words in the Australian poet Kenneth Slessor's poem titled *Sleep* that awaken atavistic memories of a birth:

"Till daylight, the expulsion and awakening,

The riving and driving forth,

Life with remorseless forceps beckoning,

Pangs and betrayal of harsh birth."

I think I can remember. I struggled being confined, there, in that ungenerous space that was so clean and sterile that I needed to consume the soil of the earth. There was no comfort in that chamber. I developed a fear of being trapped even before I had to find my way to the world that was not my mother. I wonder, is that the genesis of my panic?

Me, young, thinking about myself as I yearned to speak. The child outgrows the drawer, it was her first crib, and she begins to absorb the sounds of the planet: the groan of old timber floors, the rhythms of familiar footsteps along the hall, sounds escaping from mouths, given meaning by inflexion and by the light and expression in eyes. Before words were filed, this child knew that beauty shapes itself according to the soil on which its seed has fallen. Beauty would always be the idea that made her life tolerable.

They often found her tucked in tiny corners, surrounded by sweet-smelling heads of roses, tufts of clover she had tugged free, fragrant violets uprooted by small fists, shiny and perfectly round pebbles in her grasp. She stroked her cheek and chin with a soft, purely white chest feather from a backyard chicken.

## Next Foot Forward

She conversed in rhyme with her miniature friends in a language of her own from the time her tongue discovered four teeth. As you know, she ate colour, but her greatest love was mud. She made a mud village under the house and spent hours there with stones and flowers and stick people.

I spoke when I was nine months old, a truth straight from my mother's mouth. She did not mince words. This horrified her, as I had not yet said *Mama* or *Papa*, and besides that, she considered me an ugly baby because I was still bald. She had always wished for a child with golden curls. (My mother was somehow Victorian. To wish for golden curls when you have straight brown hair yourself, and married a swarthy, black-haired man, is very strange to my mind.)

The instance was onboard a train going from Ashfield into the city where my father worked. I was a small baby in my mother's arms. She told me I turned to the woman sitting to her left and stated quite clearly, "We are going into the city to find my father."

I have since learnt that I am neurodiverse, and suspect that was the reason my mother was unable to bond successfully with me. I was born scared. I have always feared hurting or disappointing anyone, human or creature. I hid in the broom cupboard when visitors came. I prickled, my skin and hair prickled, as though covered in ants, when certain clothes were put on me. I kicked people who tried to pat me or tell me that I was growing up. I vomited if anything remotely slimy in texture was in my food.

I remember sitting at the dining table for more than two hours after everyone had finished because I could not eat a runny egg. Every time I tried, I retched. I kicked the man who tried to take our one and only family photo when I was about three. I thought everyone saw colours around people, so I was bewildered when I was scolded for identifying a person as "that red man."

## Adelina Basile

I had distressed feelings when people seemed cruel or bad. My terrible nightmares are still discussed within our family history. I walked in my sleep and did chores, like tidying up the bookshelf, while still asleep. Once, quite recently, I awoke and found myself out on the verandah roof, so I now sleep downstairs.

Loud noises and raised voices terrified me to the point that I would climb into the broom cupboard in the hallway. I would stay there for hours, sitting on the family photo album. At present, in my neighbourhood, there are people who shout and scream in the night. They split the darkness as well as my mind and soul, and I am reduced to pulling blankets over my ears or turning on every light in my house as I struggle to breathe.

My mother would pinch my skinny upper arm when I was trying to wriggle away from people. There was not much time between when I was trying to be a child and when I got burnt, and from then on, getting through life would have been impossible without the wind and trees, dogs and wild animals of all descriptions, the light of both sun and moon, and the salt of the ocean that held me close and safe.

As I write, I am sitting on the grass in front of the Surf Life Saving Club, looking at all the incredible beauty around me as I try to capture memories.

The sedges and rushes holding the edge of the lagoon with their roots are casting shadows, long and fine, making bridges on the pool and caging in the sun.

For almost two years I have been faithful to this task. When the weather is fine, my laptop and I sit on the grassy verge in front of the surf clubhouse as I allow the world of my childhood to entice me back into security and wonder. When the mood takes me and the wind sends me a perfect wave, I leave my laptop and race down the slope. Splashing through the lagoon, I dive into the surf and duck under the water to swim out the back of the wave line.

### Next Foot Forward

My skin buzzes with iodine and excitement. They create a type of electricity that sizzles into every cell until I know myself fully. Then I hitchhike on a wave back to shore, carried like a favoured passenger. I come to rest with my chin in the wet sand and a heart lighter than air. These days are treasured.

Wandering along the rocks at low tide, as I take a break and have a stretch, I spy a boy who was probably the same age as I was when I caught fire. I squat beside the blue-ringed octopus's pool to watch him.

He was skinny, about eight or nine years old, and sitting on his heels at the edge of a rock pool. Long hours of sunlight and salt had burned his skin the brown of old nuts, with a glow of gold beneath, and his wide feet with splayed toes gripped the sharp rocks comfortably. He was munching on a sandwich, but his gaze never moved from the pool and its surroundings.

As a small crab zigzagged over a rock and hurried by his foot, he stopped chewing and stayed still, observing the crab as it found a hiding place in a small pukka. Unlike most children, this one made no move to disturb or annoy the small sea creature.

As he bent to look at a sea anemone, his head was reflected in the clear surface water. Green eyes set deeply between straight black brows were fringed by thick, dark lashes and looked like anemones themselves. The rest of his face was even-featured and serious. When he touched the anemone with a gentle forefinger, the pale of his hand flashed pink in sharp contrast to the deep brown of his skin.

For a while he remained motionless, yet his eyes constantly moved, noting the winds, the waves, and all the small movements of the pool. A smile came deep in his eyes, barely touching his lips, as he watched a small fish dart to the surface and greedily gobble the remaining crumbs from the sandwich.

**Adelina Basile**

In one graceful movement, the boy straightened, the long thin muscles of his legs pushing him upright fluidly. Then he turned and walked leisurely through the shallows, just a small boy with bony shoulders and wrists pushing sharply through the skin, who looked as if he was taking survey of his entire kingdom. He trod with high steps, feet pulling quickly up through the surface of the water without a splash, in the manner of someone used to the constant drag of the surf.

Further along the beach, a group of children were playing at the surf line, running into the retreating waves then dashing back when the water surged up the beach. Their shrill voices carried across the sand, high above the constant boom of the breaking waves. The boy stopped for a while and watched them. He stood with the water rushing around his legs, as if trying to decide what action to choose. After one long look out to sea, he started running towards the children and was soon lost in their midst.

That boy, too, has discovered the essential truth of nature. It will hold him well as he travels his path through life.

Next Foot Forward

# Chapter 31

My life was shifting again, quietly at first, like sand stirred by an unseen tide.

Okinawa in the seventies had been a haven, especially for children like Simon, who craved fresh air and freedom. The island offered days steeped in salt-scented winds and evenings laced with cicada songs. A new cardiologist had arrived on the base, bringing with him more than medical skill, he brought relief, and confidence. Simon, though still needing more rest than most boys his age, was finally beginning to walk in rhythm with his peers. It felt like the sky had unclenched just a little.

Clark and I had no passion between us, and strangely, that absence gave way to something surprisingly stable, mutual respect and a household uncluttered by emotional storms. Peaceful, even. When the orders came in October, Clark swept through the front door with a triumphant grin, waving papers like victory flags.

"Get packing!" he beamed. "We're headed to the Upper Peninsula. You'll love it, fly-fishing paradise, and one step closer to getting you back Down Under."

And just like that, life spun again. The island's soft air and still sea had been a balm, healing me from the jagged panic I suffered after Richard and I shattered so painfully apart. Now, the hush of Okinawa would be replaced by the wild edges of Michigan. A trans-Pacific leap into the unknown.

It was November when we arrived. As we drove toward the base gates at Kincheloe, the first snow began to fall, fine and quiet, like a whispered arrival. Tiny white flakes drifted around the windscreen, softening the starkness of our new world. The contrast was striking: the tropics still clung to my skin, yet here was the beginning of a long, frozen chapter.

## Adelina Basile

Kincheloe Air Force Base awaited us, a shadowed post on the borderlands, perched just outside the twin Sault Ste Maries, American and Canadian. A land of snowdrifts, strategic air command, and steel silence. Clark, ever drawn to the blinking hum of code and circuits, would begin again there. I packed up our marine collections with tender reverence, tucking away memories like seashells too delicate for the cold. He said we'd return to Australia eventually, but nothing felt certain.

I stepped out into another planet. Everything familiar dissolved into frost and foreignness. The trees were taller, the wind sharper, and the quiet more absolute. And yet, I was still me. Changed, perhaps. But not undone.

Remembering my analyst's encouragement to allow my voice and imagination to come to the fore, I now take you to the planet in my mind, a planet evoked from my first glimpse of our new base. As we came to the main gates, the November snow began to fall.

I had never seen so many pine trees marching to all points of the compass in perfectly straight lines. Our base had been plonked in the middle. I felt I was visiting a kingdom that was not yet named.

Beautiful Venusian forests reached all the way to the sky and almost didn't stop in time. I hiked out to them often, mostly when it was early enough not to bother anyone, mostly when day was breaking. The woods were like some poet might describe, with rich textures re-creating themselves forever into infinity, straight lines, or how a painter, when they're not thinking, just paints. Beautiful Venusian forests reaching all the way to the sky, right up to my face, into my eyes.

We arrived in Michigan in November. As autumn drew to a close in Michigan's Upper Peninsula, the landscape transformed into a breathtaking tapestry of nature's final flourish before winter's embrace. Picture vast Lake Superior, its edges starting to crystallise with delicate ice formations. In the early morning light, they glistened like diamonds waiting to be gathered.

The woods in late spring in the Upper Peninsula were alive with movement, a dance of light and shadow beneath the canopy.

Once the boys were settled in school, I would grab my fly rod and vest, my .44 Ruger carbine (bear country), and set out exploring. I was trying to find a stream I had caught a glimpse of earlier in the week.

The dreaded biting midges had not yet descended upon the woods. The trees, aspen, birch, and some I never learnt the names of, were bursting with full foliage, quivering in response to hidden rhythms; perhaps the whisper of the wind or the unseen touch of fleeting wings. Tiny finches, like unmoored kites, fluttered unpredictably, descending and rising again in a choreography only they understood. Above me, a red-bellied woodpecker perched, its sharp gaze turned upon my face. I was reminded of a stern music teacher, unreadable yet commanding, who rapped my knuckles with a ruler at my Saturday morning piano lesson.

Through the skinny-trunked trees (I never did get used to them, considering that I grew up under or behind the grand trunks of my Australian eucalypts), glimpses of water flickered like shifting mirrors, drawing me toward the small tributary I had stumbled upon the day before. The humid air thickened; it grasped the birdsong and suspended it in invisible strands, as if melodies could be caught and held in spider silk. The symphony of the forest was not a force, more an encouragement, inviting me to absorb myself into its chaotic beauty. Worries and yearnings dissolved into a sea of sound.

As I loosened my waterproof Canadian hiking boots, ready to cool my feet, a movement among the aspens and birch trees stilled my breath. A mother and her white-tailed fawn stepped with delicate precision, their hooves lifting like ballet dancers brushing the forest floor. They were moving the very way I had taught my boys, carefully, slowly, and silently. Their eyes met mine, silent, unwavering, before they melted back into the wilderness, quite nonchalant and unafraid. Some people find their energy in caffeine or nicotine; for me, nothing invigorates like witnessing an animal at ease in its untamed world.

With a cheese stick between my teeth, my saliva started flowing as I followed the call of memory to the pond I had glimpsed before. There it was, no more than twelve feet across, spilling into a meandering streamlet. Soft, tussocky grasses made a natural cushion on its bank. After my hour-long walk, it was a welcoming place to rest. My dangling feet just touched the surface of the water with the worn soles of my loosened boots.

As I reached for a fresh stick of jerky, the magic unfolded, a sudden, smooth ripple stretched across the surface, a silent revelation in the stillness.

Before my eyes, a beaver family emerged, two full-grown adults, a teenager, and, at last, a tiny kit. They moved effortlessly through the water, diving, rolling, gliding with an ease that made the pond seem like their personal summer retreat. For a long moment, they didn't notice me, lost in their games, their joy. I had always thought beavers were nocturnal, but here they were, alive in the daylight, embodying a rhythm of life I hadn't expected.

Then, with a sudden crack, a tail slapped the surface. A declaration. One of them, larger, confident, had seen me. He was unmistakably the patriarch. Water droplets caught the light as he wriggled towards my boots, staring, assessing. Motionless, I stared back. There was something in that whiskered face, an intelligence, a curiosity, a purity and a quiet command. Then, with unexpected mischief, he twisted and delivered a spectacular slap, sending a spray across my legs before turning, gathering his family with paternal precision, and leading them down the southern bend of the pond. There, among a chaotic tangle of wood and branches,

## Next Foot Forward

I saw that what I had stumbled upon was not just a pond, but a permanent beaver dam.

The thrill of this discovery unsettled me into an awe. I could not fish here; this was their home, their world. I was already rising to leave when, with unabashed boldness, my little beaver friend returned. He scurried back to me, nose quivering, resting against my boot. I hadn't realised until now how small his eyes were, his nose, it seemed, did all the work. His fear had vanished, replaced entirely by intrigue. And what followed? A flirtation, a dance of sorts. He rushed to deeper water, tumble-turning, smacking his tail in excitement, before scurrying back to my boot, drawn inexplicably, probably, to the scent of worn leather.

Repeatedly, he darted towards his den to check on his family, only to return without them. I think he had become jealous of me and did not want to share! He kept pressing his damp nose against my boots, as if I were part of his world now. My time and space dissolved into the ether of the sublime. I was no longer just an observer, I was at the heart of something rare, something wild and fleeting. And then, with no ceremony, he was gone. He did not return.

For all the years I spent in America, I never chased the usual landmarks. No tourist traps, no postcards to commemorate the expected. But I was flirted with by a beaver, paced alongside a lynx in the twilight, and, most of all, taught my children that nature, raw and untamed, provides all we truly need, no matter where we call home.

The trees, once ablaze with fiery reds, oranges and golds, now began to bare their bones, their skeletal branches reaching towards the sky. Their vibrant leaves carpeted the ground, creating a mosaic of rich, earthy tones and an umami scent of life's goodness. The air was crisp and invigorating, carrying the faint scent of pine and the distant whisper of winter. The trees of the Upper Peninsula were unknown to my eye, and I marvelled at their fineness. I was used to old-growth hardwood forests, and these white, whispering trees were sketched, only half formed. There were quaking aspens, white and black spruces, pines, and maple trees. They bewildered me because they marched in straight lines. Once, at the start of a big snowfall, I sought shelter in the trees and found that whichever way I looked, I would never find a landmark because all lines and rows were straight. For the first time, I was in a planted forest, and my heart became hollow with sadness. I would have loved to witness those skinny trees finding their own place to grow.

Birdsong was replaced by the gentle rustle of leaves and the soft murmur of the river. The snowy owls visited in winter, coming down from the Arctic. They were big birds with striking white plumage and could be seen on fence posts and in stubble fields. Unlike Australian owls, they hunted and fed during the day. The world felt hushed, as if holding its breath in anticipation of the next snowfall. The quality of the air was pure and sharp, each breath a reminder of the changing season, filling the lungs with a sense of anticipation.

As I wandered, picking mushrooms and berries, or just watching the clouds of butterflies, I promised myself that I would be stronger and more capable of speaking my mind when I returned home. Within my family, I was the damaged one. If we were birds, I would have been pushed out of the nest because the other siblings knew how to demand sustenance. The parent birds, so busy providing for them, found that one lost didn't matter.

It was there, in the dry and mostly freezing air, that we lived for two years until Clark was discharged and we headed back to Australia. We acquired the skills of bow and rifle hunting, ice fishing and fly fishing during our stay at Kincheloe Air Force Base, home of the great B-52 bombers. It suited my nature to be hunting, fishing and gathering for sustenance. I loved wandering in the fields at the beginning of autumn, before the leaves had turned. We meandered without haste, with no hunting dog; our eyes were sharp, focused for the flight of a ruffed grouse. We were

## Next Foot Forward

silent, using hand signals. I believe all my early childhood reading had paid off as we walked like Indians, without a sound or snap of a stick. I had taught this to the boys from the time they could walk. We made no heavy marks on our planet. We hunted with respect, in awe of the gift that nature gave us.

American woodcocks were also in abundance, but we liked eating grouse. In Michigan, we had to obtain special licences for whatever animal we wished to hunt. The fact that we challenged ourselves by using only a .410 shotgun is proof of our abilities as well as our sporting natures.

Grouse belong to the pheasant family and are shaped like a chicken. The male has fluffy white feathers around his neck and an elegant but draping tail. In a good season they are plump, so we never needed more than four when we hunted. Most of them only flock in the breeding season, so we had to work hard to catch our dinner. Often all I could see were the bobbling beanies of my sons as they moved silently through the autumnal grasses. Beautifully patterned, grouse feathers are barred in black, white and burnt sienna. Neck feathers are small and dark, while their chests are white, barred with crescents of black. The tail and flight feathers are plain. We respected the soul and memory of any animal that gave us sustenance, and I would gently skin the birds so that I could later tan and preserve them for their beauty. Grouse meat is not gamey like other wild birds; their diet of berries and plants gives a subtle but complex flavour. They are wonderful in curries or simply roasted. Like all meats, the older the bird, the slower and longer you cook it.

I learnt how to skin and preserve many different animals and would gather roadkill to respect the wildlife of that place. When we returned to Australia, I had skins of rabbit, snow rabbits (pure white), and grouse tucked into my suitcases.

Some considered it a harsh place to live, but we seemed to adjust our bodies from warm coral water temperatures to wind chills of minus sixteen, with absolute enjoyment. Imagine a crisp winter day by the river, where the air is filled with the promise of adventure. Simon was bundled up in a bright red snowsuit. Damian, in his green snowsuit and purple beanie, was hunting and netting butterflies further down the river embankment.

This was our first time fly fishing. Simon stood at the water's edge, his breath visible in the frigid air. His eyes were wide with excitement as he gripped his fishing rod, yelling, "Mother! Clark! I think I've got one!" The line was taut and dancing with the struggle of what we later found was a thirty-two-pound king salmon. The air was deliciously crisp and tasted like green apples as we fished beside that small tributary of the St Mary's River.

The river, partially frozen at the edges, flowed steadily in its centre, its surface shimmering under the pale winter sun. Simon's cheeks were flushed with the cold and the thrill of the catch. His gloved hands worked tirelessly, reeling in the line with determination and vigour. We had a rule: "You catch it, you land it." So we put our rods down and watched his struggle. His fishing line's breaking strain was only twelve pounds, so he would need to use his brain as well as finesse.

For twenty minutes, the battle ensued. The salmon, a magnificent thirty-two-pound beast, fought valiantly, its powerful body slicing through the water, sending sprays of icy droplets into the air. The world seems to hold its breath when you are inside nature. The occasional call of a bird and the soft crunch of snow underfoot were the only sounds that accompanied the rhythmic whir of his reel. Onlookers, fishermen from further up the river, were drawn down by our shouts of encouragement. They gathered at a respectful distance, enjoying this boy-and-fish spectacle.

Finally, with a triumphant shout, Simon pulled the salmon ashore. The fish glistened in the winter light, its scales a mosaic of silver and blue. While I was recalling the mullet scales on my seashore

## Next Foot Forward

back in Australia, Simon whispered, "Mother, I wet myself!" What a testament to my son's perseverance.

Once we were settled, the boys were enrolled in the third school of their small lives. As soon as they were on the school bus, I would grab my fly rod and tackle box, as well as my .44 calibre Ruger carbine. The firearm was essential as I explored wild places where bears roamed. I was used to tracking animals but got the shock of my life when I saw the bear scratches high up on tree trunks, far taller than myself.

Bowhunting was my favourite season, not because I was good with the bow, but because as winter began its slow descent onto northern Michigan and the Great Lakes started to make ice on their edges, I entered a capsule of absolute quiet. This was a time for me to embrace the gentle skin of silence that wafted upon me and gave me a clarity and peace like no other. I never had a panic attack when we were snowbound, and I was so far away from parents and siblings. Kincheloe Air Force Base had been a Strategic Air Command base during the Cold War and was being phased out. We survived the famous snow of January 1978 before we left.

Our farewell from America was full of drama. Chicago had the closest Australian Embassy, where we were able to have our various papers stamped and verified. I found the Art Institute in Chicago. They were celebrating some hundred-year anniversary with the artist Chagall, and there, at the entrance to the museum, were three of Chagall's free-standing windows alive with the most voluptuous, blazing colours imaginable. The mixture of colours shocked the breath from my lungs. That was my one and only exploration of the urban part of the United States, as I had stayed safely in the natural environment with the beavers, bears, skunks, mushrooms, berries, and tiny little biting midges during the summer.

We had to leave the peninsula in a blizzard, in a small plane called a "Snow Goose." It had two engines and a type of radiator on each wing. The flight was a bumpy one, as the wheels did not go up after take-off because the pilot was worried he could not get them back down. By this time in my life, I had tablets to take to overcome the onset of a panic attack but was terrified to find that we were landing at O'Hare Airport in Chicago, in a white-out. There was an extended wait in the big jet until visibility improved, and then we were airborne and on our way to San Francisco. We were all grumpy and hungry, but because we were always heading west, breakfast never came.

Damian had a favourite toy throughout his life, a green stuffed frog called Fred. Each time we moved to a new place, I embroidered the name of the place for him. Consequently, Freddie's entire soft body was covered with my elaborate stitching. We had a long wait for our flight to Sydney, and in the middle of the concourse, Damian threw himself on his back in a terrible tantrum of despair and grief, screaming, "I forgot Fred!"

This poor little boy was filled with geographical anxiety because of my choices. He had endured ten bedrooms in his young life. Whenever I had to move house, his question was always the same: "Where will my bed be?" and "Will I have a window?"

Prior to our departure from Michigan, we were staying in a motel, and Damian had perched Fred on a windowsill. There was no consoling this little boy. I had to phone back to the motel and speak to the owner, who went along to the room and found Fred. Damian had to hear the words with his own ears. I asked if Fred could be packed and sent to my parents' address in Taree, NSW, Australia. Again, Damian had to hear the man say he would. We then boarded a Qantas plane to cross the Pacific Ocean once again, for home.

Next Foot Forward

# Chapter 32

Autumn, 27 March 1978, was a bright day in Australia. The sky was nothing like the timid canopy of the northern hemisphere. After the weak, grey winter of northern Michigan, the blaze of blue above Sydney was powerful, almost dazzling, as we landed at Sydney International Airport and were greeted by my parents and some of my family. The air was sweet-smelling, and there was space around me in a way I'd forgotten existed after seven years without it.

Damian's frog, Fred, was already at my parents' place! After visiting relations and showing Clark around Sydney, we headed north. A few days later we were back at the beach shack, just before the mullet began to run for the year.

About a kilometre from the beach, tucked within the densely forested bush, was a house for sale on twenty-six acres. I was determined to get settled so the boys could enrol in school; I knew they were behind Australian standards. I had saved every penny I'd ever earned and kept it in an Australian bank account, along with the boys' child endowment payments from the government. It was a sizeable amount, enough for a deposit on the property. My boys had grown up with space and wilderness, and I believed that was why Simon's heart had remained stable. After his surgery, I had been told it would be wise for him to live in an unindustrialised environment. The beach and the bush seemed perfect for us.

During the 1970s in Australia, it was almost impossible for a single woman to get a home loan. I had quickly found a teaching position at a parish school in the nearest town, about a twenty-five-minute drive away. I persisted with various bank managers and, thanks to my savings, eventually secured the loan. The repayments came to three-quarters of my salary, so I knew we'd be hunting and fishing for protein and growing everything else. As Clark and I had agreed, I bought the house in my name, expecting him to head off to his dream destination, the Great Barrier Reef. He had his military pension and the payments he received for having three dependants. I didn't begrudge him that, but I was desperate to begin life again.

Mother's kitchen smelled of garlic and sea salt, her usual offering of comfort. Clark sat at the table, laughing too loudly at one of her stories, his hand lingering a little too long on her wrist as she poured his wine. She giggled, well, simpered really, and my stomach twisted. We were playing a round of Canasta.

My father got up to stretch and stood by the window, polishing his glasses with the hem of his shirt, pretending not to notice. He had always been the peacekeeper, the quiet bridge between storms. But even he looked tired.

Clark had become a fixture in their home, slipping into their routines like a stray cat who'd learned which door to scratch. He talked shells with my father, rare specimens, trade routes, the value of the collection we'd built together. He'd borrowed money to buy exotic pieces from overseas, and my father, ever the enthusiast, had obliged.

I watched Clark charm them both, my mother beaming at his compliments on her cooking, my father nodding along as Clark spun stories of reef dives and mollusc taxonomy. They were enchanted. I was exhausted.

He no longer wanted to move north to the Barrier Reef as we had planned. Our communication had grown strained, clipped. The agreement we had made, the one that had secured him permanent residency, was fading before my eyes. I reminded him of it, gently at first, then with increasing urgency.

"You promised," I said one evening, standing in the hallway as he zipped up his leather jacket.

He shrugged. "Things change."

## Next Foot Forward

He had abandoned a family in America long before I met him. I hadn't known that then. Now I could see the pattern. He liked attention. He liked being wanted. And my parents, probably worn down by my own complexities, seemed relieved to have someone else to focus on.

My mother pleaded with me.

"He's good for you," she said, clutching my hand. "He's settled. He's clever."

I wanted to scream. Instead, I nodded and walked away.

My father tried to mediate, offering quiet suggestions and half-hearted compromises. But the tension only thickened. The house felt like a stage set for a play I'd never auditioned for.

Then one morning, Clark rolled into the driveway on a motorbike. He grinned, helmet under his arm, and said, "I'm heading north."

That was it. No goodbye. No discussion.

We filed for divorce, just as the contract had outlined. A clean break, on paper at least.

But the mess lingered. It sat in the shells, in the wine glasses, in the echo of my mother's laughter.

Our house had two bedrooms and sat well back from the road inside a hardwood forest. A dirt driveway wound its way through grey and mahogany eucalypts, and beyond them stood a wall of casuarinas where black cockatoos settled before rain. At certain times during the night, a deep growling and terrifying screech would tear from one end of the block to the other. We eventually learned it was male koalas on the prowl during mating season.

Behind the house was a clear paddock where, each afternoon, a mob of red-necked wallabies grazed, lounged about, and scratched their chests, while the females loosened their pouches and allowed their joeys a nibble and a romp. I bought a book on subsistence farming and began planting all our seasonal vegetables. The ground was hard and barely worked, but everything grew.

Next Foot Forward

# Chapter 33

While teaching third grade, the curriculum required me to teach a five-week block on nutrition for children. We built the food pyramid in class: breads, pasta and cereals, 40%; fruit and vegetables, 35%; meat and fish, 20%; oils and fats, 5%. It didn't take me long to realise that our own diet was rather lacking in high-quality protein, so I went home that night determined to hunt for some.

Not wanting to expose the boys to my idiosyncrasies, I waited until they were asleep, grabbed my .22 single-shot rifle and skinning knife, and headed up to the top paddocks with a headlamp strapped across my forehead. A half-moon lit the world, casting fairytale-blue shadows and making me feel as though I'd stepped into the animated film *Watership Down*, which I'd watched with the boys in the seventies. With the earthy smell of swamp oaks and wattle thick around me, I felt like the first person ever to set foot on that small plot of land.

The wallabies were nowhere in sight. As I scoured the perimeter, I startled a group of kookaburras who lifted off and settled on a nearby stump. While watching them, I noticed a goanna, sometimes called a monitor lizard, resting beside a fallen log. Naturally, there was nothing in my *Self-Sufficiency* book about goannas; it had been written by an English author, John Seymour.

Still, I was on a mission. I thought that if I could get it, kill it and dress it before the boys knew, I could cook it and pretend it was a large flathead fillet.

The shot was easy, but the skinning was so exhausting I feared I wouldn't finish before it was time for work. Under the pale half-moon, I dispatched the goanna as gently and reverently as I could, but bits of blood and fat flicked into my hair and across my face, unsettling me for the act I was performing. Eventually, I had two large tail fillets, which did resemble flathead, and I laid them carefully in the refrigerator. Before I could shower and collapse into bed, I had to fetch a shovel and spade from the shed to bury the remains.

Marinated and cooked with beans and tomatoes, we ate it the following evening. My sons, so loyal to me, ate without complaint. I thought it was vile, and have since learnt from my Indigenous friends that it should have been roasted in its skin over an open fire.

That horrible experience sent me searching for another way to provide meat regularly for the boys. On Mondays, at the saleyards in the large town nearby, animals and produce were auctioned, sold or traded. Farmers and primary producers arrived with every type of animal and bird imaginable. I'd taken on some well-paid local tutoring after school to raise money, and when the school holidays began, the boys and I drove into the market looking for something we could raise on our land, animals that would be comfortable in the fenced yard we had half-concreted near the top water faucet.

We came home with three fat, rosy ten-week-old piglets. I felt confident with pigs, as John Seymour's book contained a good chapter on raising and slaughtering them. I would be guided. And to anyone who wants a pet and has the space, do yourself a favour and get a pig.

Our pigs still had their milk teeth and were easily weaned; they settled quickly into our lifestyle. They had plenty of grass and herbs to nibble, and we fed them from our garden, especially carrots, sweet potato and cabbage leaves. Their favourite treat was milk, and as I always had leftover cow's milk from our first farm animals, they grew fast and beautifully healthy.

Pigs are like dogs, trusting, friendly, and playful. We'd known from the start that we were raising them for our own sustenance, but that didn't deter us from the love and fun we shared with them. When we arrived home from school, we'd unlock their yard and

## Next Foot Forward

play with them. They adored our dogs, but their favourite thing of all was being hosed with a strong jet of water. They grew quickly and grew huge. By the Christmas holidays, I knew I would have to slaughter them. A butcher further up the road could make my hams, bacon and chops, but the responsibility for the killing was mine. It was illegal for an abattoir to slaughter for an unlicensed hobby farmer.

The traditional way to kill a pig is to stick it in the throat. While I see nothing wrong with killing animals for meat, I see everything wrong with making them suffer in any way. If we kill an animal, we should do so instantaneously, with the creature having no inkling that anything unpleasant is about to happen. I led one pig at a time away from the yard, shot it in the head with a .22, and bled it instantly, just as we bled tailor and salmon the minute, we beached them. With a rifle, you can stand well back, aim at the pig's brain, and the animal has no idea before it is stone dead.

During the winter school holidays we had built a large outdoor barbecue in the yard, and I had a huge copper full of water heating. I'd read that the scraping of the skin was done with a piece of old tin, so I simply took the top off a tin of tomatoes with the opener.

The boys and I heaved the pig into the wheelbarrow, trundling him down the track with half his body hanging over the side. They were truly large pigs. By sheer good luck, the water was at the perfect temperature, because scraping the skin turned out to be the easiest part of the whole process.

From then on, we followed our self-sufficiency book word for word. Pulleys and ropes had been rigged up in the carport the night before, and with great difficulty we managed to hang the pig. Simon held the book, reading aloud. He and I can control our senses enough to get the nasty jobs done. Damian, with his extremely developed sense of smell and taste, was of a very different temperament.

Simon was thirteen, and Damian fourteen months younger. His job was to dig a big hole down the front yard, and when the innards came out, he was to wheel them down in the barrow and bury them.

I cut and sawed and did exactly as Simon instructed. But when I opened the belly, the pile of steaming innards tumbled out over all of us. While Damian retched, we gathered the entrails into the wheelbarrow.

"Off you go," I said to him. With his face turned away from the coils of intestine and stomach, he stumbled down the track towards the hole.

A terrible smell wafted across the farm because Simon had forgotten to read a line that said, *do not pierce the rectum*. Halfway down the track, Damian tripped on a big black butt root and once again the guts spilled across the ground. My poor son burst into tears and ran off to hide from the awful deed his mother was performing.

My kitchen bench was six feet long, so was the side of the pig. Once you're inside a body, there are clear lines of tendon and muscle, and it is quite beautiful to see, and satisfying to dismember an animal cleanly. But it was mid-summer, and butchering is exhausting work. With two more pigs still to process, I rang the petrol station and asked if they could deliver some ice. The fridge and freezer were overflowing.

By the time I got to the third pig, I was too exhausted to move and my arm could no longer hold a blade. My whole body was dripping with sweat, and I later found out I had lost four kilograms. The boys filled our full-sized bath with ice, carried the pig inside, and laid it in the tub. It was so long that its head rested against the wall at the shower end, facing its clean little trotters at the other.

At that moment, my parents' car pulled up. My mother burst through the front door with some mail, calling out, "I just need to use the toilet, Lina!" The toilet was next to the bathroom.

## Next Foot Forward

A tremendous shriek echoed down the hall as she stepped into the bathroom to wash her hands.

"Look what you've done, Lina! Now you've got a pig in the bath! I am never coming here again!" she cried, scurrying back to the car.

I watched from the doorway as she launched into exaggerated hand and head movements, explaining to my father exactly what his daughter had been up to.

That Christmas, I gave hams to my brothers and sisters. And after the butcher had finally taken all the meat and packaged it properly, we would open the freezer and simply stare at the mountain of meat we no longer wanted to eat.

We did have wonderful survival skills. Despite my fraught relationship with my mother, I was developing a sense of myself. Nature was the one constant in my life and had become my quiet mentor. Observing it calmed me, gave me a sense of permanence and security. Trees protected me as much as they sheltered other creatures. They gave me shade. Birds lifted my heart as they arrowed across the sky.

The tides came and went, forming a steady pattern that soothed me. My sons shared that same entrancement with the natural world, and I already knew they would become champions of the environment we all cherished.

I was excited to return to teaching at the Forster Catholic school. After assembly, where I was introduced to the children during the eleven o'clock recess, I came face to face with my nightmare.

The schoolyard shimmered under the sun, cicadas shrieking from the gums like a warning. I stood at the edge of my classroom, checking off the names of my pupils, half-listening to the hum of children. Then I saw him.

The priest.

### Adelina Basile

He moved through the crowd like a ghost dressed in black, his collar stark against the soft folds of his neck. That face, round, flushed. Those blue eyes, too bright. They had haunted my sleep for years. I froze. The clipboard slipped from my fingers and clattered onto the concrete.

No one noticed.

My breath vanished. The world narrowed to a pinpoint, and I was nine again, lying in a sickbed, the smell of antiseptic and stale sheets rising like ghosts around me. I couldn't speak. I couldn't move. The sun was too bright. The air too thick.

That evening, I collapsed. One of the parents who had known me from Sunday masses gathered me up and drove me to the hospital. She asked no questions.

The hospital room was white and humming. Machines blinked softly beside me. A nurse adjusted my IV and smiled gently, as though I were just another tired teacher who'd pushed too hard. The doctor came and went, his words floating above me like mist.

"Nervous breakdown," he said. "Rest. Four days."

He didn't know. How could he?

Fifteen years had passed. I'd lived oceans away. And yet here he was, this predator, still cloaked in the Church's silence, shuffled from parish to parish like a dirty secret. Even New Guinea hadn't been far enough.

I stared at the ceiling tiles, counting them like prayers. My voice was gone again. My body, a cage. My life, a circle.

Next Foot Forward

# Chapter 34

To thrive on our twenty-six acres, we needed books. My bookshelf was overflowing with our books. Plato's *Republic* settled happily beside the many books on self-sufficiency along with the classics, *Lays of Ancient Rome*, and fiction. We also overflowed with maps, manuals, and all manner of catalogues advertising agricultural or gardening products. If my car needed a service, my sons found a manual. Necessity had enabled us to feel confident in any situation. I loved my Nubian goats who cavorted as though they were puppies. And clever they were. They climbed on each other's shoulders as they ate all the plants I had hanging under my eaves. Once, when I came home from school, there was a note taped on my mailbox. "Lina. Your goats are tied up at the top farm. They have eaten the gardens of the entire village!" Such joyful, happy creatures gave me a great deal of pure happiness.

I was learning that I functioned very well on this earth but floundered when trying to understand what people wanted. I was great in the urgent doing of things but woeful in deciphering what people meant. When my body became tired and my mind was stressed, I was ripe for the panic attacks to climb through my vagal system and wreak havoc with my emotions. I thought of them like an octopus whose mouth was deep in my belly while its tentacles touched and sucked at every cell of my limbic system.

Simon headed into puberty. His heart started impinging on his life and by the time the bus brought him home from school, he pretty much ate and went to bed. He was not allowed to do any sports at school and the teachers were all aware of the necessity of having his medical file on hand. I became incensed when I discovered that on the weekly sports day, Simon was given the job of wandering all over the school picking up trash and determined that we would overcome this problem.

I cast my mind for some outdoor activity that would allow him to rest and decided that he should learn to surf. Such a silly mother as I chose the one thing that, as well as exhausting him, kept him healthy. I bought a blank, which is just a big piece of foam, roughly shaped, and he and I together shaped and made his first board. The father of one of my students was a surfboard manufacturer. I went to him for hints on board making and once we had finished it, he took it and did a great paint job on it. The southern end of our beach makes for fantastic waves when a big swell comes from the south. Board riders came from all along the coast when the point was working.

Those beautiful boys and girls paid attention as I lectured them on what to do if Simon should have a heart stoppage or attack while out on his board. They knew he had to be resuscitated out on his board while another rider should paddle to shore and call the ambulance. My admiration for young people, even in this day, knows no bounds. They are serious-minded beings who listen and act when necessary. The future of the world is quite safe in the hands of our future adults. My heart swells with admiration and love for them.

## Chapter 35

Meanwhile, Damian had become a child of the bush and spent hours wandering through our acres, observing with the eye of a scientist, or a jeweller, which he now is. He revelled in dangerous weather. The storm had roared into being with a fury that made the ground tremble beneath us. Rain lashed against the windows, lightning clawed at the sky, and the wind howled through the eucalypts like a wild animal unleashed. Inside the house, Simon and I had done all we could, secured the animals, lit the candles, and braced ourselves for the long night ahead. But as we settled in, I suddenly realised something was missing. Someone was missing.

Damian. I was scared.

Panic surged through me like the crackling energy in the storm itself. The house was small—there were few places to hide—and yet he was nowhere to be found. My pulse quickened as I called his name, my voice barely rising above the relentless hammering of the rain on the tin roof. No answer. I grabbed the torch and staggered out into the wild chaos beyond the door, nearly tripping over Storm Boy, our Chow, who was trembling and frothing, huddled inside his own black fur.

The wind threatened to pull me back, whipping my hair into a frenzy, the rain drenching me in an instant. I fought forward, calling his name repeatedly, my voice swallowed by the roar of nature. My boots sank into the mud as I made my way up toward the top paddock, my breath coming in short gasps as fear coiled tighter in my chest. Then, in the yellow glow of my torch beam, I saw him.

Damian sat on a lone stump in the open grass, utterly still, utterly mesmerised. Lightning split the sky above him, illuminating his silhouette, small yet unshaken, as he gazed at the storm with the awe of a scientist and the reverence of an artist. He was drenched, the rain soaking his clothes, his hair plastered to his forehead, yet he did not flinch. The world was raging around him, but he was lost in its beauty.

My breath caught, anger and relief colliding inside me. I roused on him, my voice sharp, urgent, trembling with the echoes of my terror. He turned his face towards me, utterly unbothered, his eyes still filled with wonder.

"I just wanted to see how it all worked, Mother," he said.

Of course. Of course he did.

Meanwhile, Clark, always the opportunist, slithered back into our lives. He had managed to go up to the reef as per our agreement. I did not know that somehow he was living in the Magnetic Island house and running his charter boat business from there. We did not have a postal service, so I used to pick up all our mail and deliver it to my parents, as necessary. I noticed his writing on an envelope addressed to them and stood by while they read it. The hide of him. He had severely misjudged my parents. He offered them a "deal." He would "buy" the house from them at twenty dollars a week if they would put the title in his name and in return he would do any maintenance. That lit my mother's anger and finally she gave up on her dream. She was furious and as quickly as possible called her solicitor, got the house on the market up north, and sold it.

# Chapter 36

There was no communication with Clark after that, even though he owed my father a great deal of money for the specimen shells that had gone into Clark's scientific collection. My father was left with invoices from all around the world for rare specimen shells that he bought on Clark's behalf, thinking he was a silent partner in this shell trading business. In my entire life, I have never heard my father complain about another person. He told me once that his biggest regret was that he did not take his mother to the movie theatre as much as he could have. This from a ninety-nine-year-old man who had been supporting his family since he was twelve.

When my parents sold the house in town, they had decided to build another house next to the beach shack, so they used to pass my driveway every day. Both were dangerous on the road, so I offered to drive them to Mass every Saturday night. While I loved the warmth and connection that I felt during the Mass, my mother was constant in her criticisms of everything. My hair, clothes, the state of the boys' hair, my single life, and "why can't you be like the others?" That latter one tossed me into bewilderment as I had no desire to be like anyone but my own self.

Gradually I developed a social phobia as well as my panic attacks and my life became very narrow. As far as possible, I tried to ensure that we went to the many family celebrations which were all over the state and required extended periods of driving, as I wanted my sons to know their uncles, aunt, and cousins. We were quite a large family. One school holiday I had promised to take the boys to Sydney to visit their cousins. We had packed the night before and set out early, a few hours before sunrise, but had only driven for about forty-five minutes when I suffered a severe bout of diarrhoea on the side of the road and then I just disintegrated into a gibbering mess. I felt that I was about to die, my mouth was so dry I could not spit and an utter dread overcame my soul.

**Adelina Basile**

I turned the car around and told the boys how sorry I was, and we drove straight back to the beach where my parents were just up for breakfast. I felt as limp as a dying pup. That was the first time my mother had seen me in such a state. She scolded me while my father made me a cup of tea. "Why didn't you let someone else drive?" asked my mother. That moment I felt the panes in my heart crack, and I realised that after all the years of her interference, she had never once even considered that I had no one to help me. How could she? She had been driven everywhere whenever she needed. I took the boys home and as we had breakfast, for the first time I told them of my panic disorder. They, with absolute equanimity, hugged me and said, "We know, Mother."

Next Foot Forward

# Chapter 37

Life for the boys was fine. They had a school bus full of friends, the bush with the permanent wallabies, gliders, possums, goannas and birds, and as well as their farm chores, they had the beach with its unpolluted water and matchless sand. Damian had become an excellent free diver and was working on his first spear gun. We had the cow artificially inseminated and were awaiting a calf; I was making our yoghurt, ice cream and ricotta, as well as growing all our seasonal vegetables. A flock of laying hens helped us keep the grass down and we moved them from place to place with a portable coop. I had acquired a mob of geese who were immensely entertaining. They wandered around importantly behind the big gander and were exceptionally efficient at keeping the coarser native grasses under their control. We did not need a fence for those geese. All it took was to buy some extra hoses and lay them on the ground. The geese never once crossed the hoses. Damian thought it might be because they were wary of snakes, of which there were many.

At one stage I had been tricked into agisting a racehorse, supposedly for six months, for a fee. Truly, I did anything for an extra dollar. Interest rates had skyrocketed on my mortgage payments and were sitting at seventeen per cent. At the end of every fortnight, I had exactly eleven dollars left. It was for my petrol for the next two weeks. The horse was a stallion and quite dangerous, nearly killing Damian, who thought that he might try to make friends with it. None of us had any experience with horses at all. When I found out it was a stolen horse, I got rid of it quickly and never again offered to look after anyone else's animals.

At night I gazed at the stars hoping to get through to the next day. My heart would be overtaken, almost consumed, by the beauty above my house. Viewing was perfect as there were no neighbours nor ambient light to dim the starlight. The tree trunks rose all around like great black stalks, straight as matches, all lit on the top by the stars. Certain times of the year, great flocks of flying foxes would darken the entire sky above as they travelled to their next roosting site. The times I spent with nature were really my only times without some form of responsibility. Panic attacks happened in the weirdest of places. Once, I was food shopping and was overcome with the dread, the terror, of what to some people must sound ridiculous, and found myself crouched on the floor of the toilets of a McDonald's restaurant. I had never even been there or known where the restrooms were.

The only way to describe an attack is to say that you are experiencing the beginning of death. The worst of it all is the fact that when you are back in your normal, intelligent mind, you are filled with shame and guilt. You are bewildered because you know that your body has tricked your mind. I tried to hide these attacks because on one occasion, my father happened to see me like that and he became quite distraught. In fact, I did not face any of my traumas or seek professional help until after my father's death.

Back under our blackbutt "widow makers" (the slang name for these trees, famous for dropping very heavy branches, thus creating widows), the boys and I bartered for most of our needs and were always on the lookout for something to fatten and sell. It was fun being a subsistence farmer. Wattle trees open their blossoms in late winter and the heady aroma of their scent filled the paddocks on our place. Being used to looking for tiny cowrie shells in the rocky sea shelves of Okinawa, my eyes searched the tough native grasses that whispered on the surface of this clay soil. If you were sharp-eyed enough and patient, you could find tiny wild orchids, tough and headstrong, forcing their delicate selves through that sunbaked clay. Most common were the spider orchids, coloured spectacularly with complex patterning on their long and skinny petals.

One year in spring, I decided to buy two dozen turkey chicks and fatten them on our free-range acres. I traded fresh chicken eggs for the turkey feed. They were the stupidest animals with which I have ever dealt. Rain pelted down one afternoon. I ran up to the paddock

## Next Foot Forward

to check on them as they were grazing. There they were, soaking wet with their heads through the fence grazing seeds. Heads like stuck piano keys. Seemingly frozen in fear, they did not know how to pull their necks back. However, they fattened up beautifully, and I sold them all for Christmas and had enough money to pay a carpenter to make a bookshelf that covered my entire fireplace wall.

I was regaining the me that had been whittled away by circumstances. Maslow is so right. You cannot self-actualise until you are secure in shelter and food. Glory is a word I learned as a small child. I learned it in relation to God and creation and other magical spiritual things. It has always been a word without a visual for me. I could never see "glory".

I had been a "glory-seeker" most of my life but lacked the tools. Now I watch the dawn, the rivers, the hanging mist wrapping the eucalypt foliage like a shawl, the sky and trivial things like raindrops. I smile at the glory of it all.

## Chapter 38

While I was busy teaching, farming and attending to children, my retired parents had a new house built behind their now empty beach shack, which was only about two kilometres down the road from me (the shack I was never allowed to live in). One Sunday my father phoned, "Come quickly Lina. Your mother has collapsed!"

Twitching and convulsing on the floor, she had lost her speech. I could tell just by looking at her that it did not seem to be a stroke, and while the ambulance was called, I began to ponder on her strange behaviour in the last two years, since we had come back from America. The weird choices she had made were not characteristic of her former self, and the nastiness she seemed to have developed was also a behaviour that was new. She had been harsh to me, viciously harsh, but never nasty in the past. As well, she had always made clever choices when money was concerned, and the buying of a house up on the Barrier Reef was unwise by any standards. I suspected that she had a tumour.

The hospital emergency room thought it was a stroke. Our hospital was not geared up to admit or treat her. My mind went into overdrive as I tried to sort out the action that I would need to take. Father had gone into silent shock. My sister and two brothers all had businesses down in the city and I knew that they found it difficult to deal with intrusions into their routines, so I knew I would have to be the one to take care of our father. He needed to be with her.

Mother was flown to Sydney in an air ambulance, enduring eleven convulsions in the flight, we later learnt. I had to organise the boys to stay with a family who lived along our road. We had met during Sunday Masses. My father, who had the softest heart in the world, had disintegrated into pieces to the point that he could not find his underwear drawer and was quite incapable of driving to the city.

## Next Foot Forward

Urgent tests at St Vincent's Hospital in Sydney revealed the truth: it was a tumour. Aggressive, unforgiving. By the time we saw her settled into the hospital bed, it had already pushed her left eye halfway out of its socket. She still couldn't speak, but the blazing anger in her eyes told me she was fully aware of how grotesque her appearance had become.

She could write, though. And she did—forcefully, with purpose. She scribbled a note and handed it to me: "Get your father to put me on the list for spare parts." Her meaning was unmistakable. She wanted to donate her organs. Another note followed: "I am sure that my kidneys and eyes are perfect and could help someone."

I admired her then more than ever. This feisty, forceful woman, glaring with her bulging eye at her two sons and husband, who stood speechless, helpless and hopeless at organising her wishes. Fear had undone them. In our family, the Italian gene incapacitated males in times of strife and confusion. Luckily, they had me.

Immediate surgery was scheduled for five a.m. the next morning. None of my brothers had the courage to speak to the doctor. So it was left to me. Her piercing blue eyes watched me, demanding obedience. I went. I told the doctor what she wanted. I made sure her wishes were known.

Then I kissed her goodbye.

I had never seen my mother in hospital before. Never even sick. Not a cold. Not a cough. And now, here she was—facing surgery, facing death, and still thinking of others.

Father and I stayed at his brother's house at Croydon Park, a suburb in the city. His brother Vince had served in New Guinea in World War II when he was nineteen. When he came home from the war, Vince's skin colour was green and he had malaria, which caught up with him throughout his life. This uncle also had nervous breakdowns and once had to leave his wife and three little children and come and live with us in the country for his health. Understandably! He had only been a month-old baby when their father was killed and, as my Nonna lost all her milk from the shock of her husband's death, my uncle Vince was, in my father's words, 'as skinny as a starving rabbit'. I found out years later that Uncle Vince thought that my father was his papa!

He would never march on Anzac Day and caused me to have nightmares by telling me of his time under fire in the war. He said he was carrying three small children across a river in New Guinea and had to stay in the water for many hours. He also told me that he saw the Japanese soldiers capture an Aussie and force a hose down his throat and then fill him with water. Then they would roll him over a wooden barrel until his stomach broke inside.

These were my favourite aunt and uncle. These brothers were Sicilian. Both had nervous dispositions and were great gentle sooks. At four the next morning, I awoke and tried to wake my father in the other bed. He pulled his blanket down until only his terrified brown eyes were showing and gasped to me through his sheet that he was having a blood pressure attack. I could see he was in a real panic, so I went into my uncle's room and tapped him awake.

'Uncle. It is time for us to go to the hospital, but father is having a blood pressure attack.'

Uncle Vince clutched his chest and turned to Aunty Maria and hoarsely cried, 'Maria, call the doctor, quickly. I think I am having a heart attack and Victor's blood pressure is out of control.'

She rang their family doctor, who seemed used to such dramatics, while I went alone to sit and wait and pray that my mother's surgery would be successful. To this day I do not know why the others did not come.

Sitting there, waiting for the outcome of my mother's surgery, I relived Simon's surgery in my mind. I had taken it upon myself to

## Next Foot Forward

learn everything I could about the human body and especially the heart, so I understood what the doctors were trying to do. I also kept up to date in First Aid with St John Ambulance. Maybe everyone thought that I was competent, seeing that I had experienced hospitals and doctors throughout my life.

My mother, on the other hand, could not even tell you where her lungs or liver were in her body. She had no interest. She seemed to have an iron-willed conviction that someone would fix her or whatever was wrong in her life. That is what I mean by her being a force. True to form, she sailed through difficult surgery and rehabilitation. For as long as I can remember, mother sailed forward on high heels (made of leather, in Italy) and never took a step back.

We had double timber driveway gates at our house and one day, after she had got her driver's licence, she reversed out of our driveway and down the main street. My father received a phone call at his work. He was told that mother was dragging both gates through the town. She was totally unaware and was never fazed, not even when she would run over one of our pets.

She made frequent buying trips to the city and flew from our local aerodrome. One afternoon our home phone rang and, when I answered, it was a woman from the telephone exchange telling me to turn the oven down to low. It seems mother had remembered while in the air, assumed the pilot had a phone, and walked up, tapped the pilot on the shoulder, and gave him our number and the request for the stove to be turned down. Once, when she was scolding me for helping some needy person, I suggested that sometimes she should try to walk in another person's shoes. 'My feet don't fit,' was her speedy reply, which left me stunned. Like everything else in her life, my mother sailed through surgery and rehabilitation with the fierce stubbornness that undid my soul so often.

… Adelina Basile

# Chapter 39

Today, there is no beach left. The eighteenth of May 2025 has now set a new flood record. Since the 1880s, when data was first recorded in our area, never has our floodplain and river delta been reduced to such inundation. My entire council area is flooded and we are isolated. My planet is severely displeased with us and I agree with it. Climate change, driven by our greedy human activities such as burning fossil fuels and deforestation, has led to this dire situation. There is such a significant increase in the frequency and intensity of natural disasters that our Bureau of Meteorology cannot find models fast enough to prepare us in a timely way. Rising global temperatures have resulted in more severe heatwaves, prolonged droughts, devastating bushfires, and floods. Each time it happens, whether fire or flood, we are told it is a 'once in a hundred years' event. The trouble is, they are happening like an invading force, every few years. Melting polar ice caps and glaciers also contribute to rising sea levels and frightful erosion.

These two weeks of being unable to rest in the ocean and squint at the sky have been filled with bushwalks through our littoral rainforests that enclose the village. Our littoral rainforests are considered so important that all the small pockets of them along the coast of New South Wales are recognised as Endangered Ecological Communities under a Threatened Species Act. I love taking a book and sitting inside one of the low thickets within the forest. Some tree species will grow stunted and slanting, while in better protected sites there are tall trees draped with vines or lianas. My headland's soils are clay and grow tough plants such as Brush Box, Water Gums and Tuckeroo. Coastal banksias border the leeward sides of our littoral rainforests and throw up tall wide flowers, yellow brushes strong enough to scrub one's toilet. These plants rely on fire for their seeds to germinate. Smelling the earthy, sour leaf litter as I read fills me with a sense of eternity. One inquisitive swamp wallaby, deep charcoal in colour and shaped

## Next Foot Forward

like a sturdy little triangular prism, stomps into view and stops, stares with such an unwavering gaze that I feel guilt rising in my soul, then turns and thumps away.

My beach is gone. Strewn as far as the furthest headland are trees, timber, fish traps and lobster pots, randomly sprawling in the yellow foam. Halfway along the beach, almost in front of the eagles' roosting tree, are two great bloated sacks of fur that were once Friesian dairy cows. The only bright colour in my world today are the two yellow ear tags of those poor cows, who would have been flung from the river ten kilometres north and then drowned as the currents carried them south. Dead cattle have washed up on all our beaches and we are unable to swim due to the toxicity of the water. Many farms were totally inundated and, as a result, the septic systems have further polluted our waters. The latest unofficial count of dead and drowned cows is possibly one thousand and two hundred. They suspect many more.

Finally, I am permitted to swim each day again. At last! The cold salty water is the one salve that relieves these damaged legs of mine. Once they are sorted, I can let my eyes and ears engage with the wonders of a surf, a beach and a wave.

My coastline has changed, as the flooding rains gathered up the sand and dunes and flung them out to sea. A sandbar or shelf has been created about three hundred metres out in the bay at the southern end. Wavelets are breaking like curling strands of vanilla icing on a cake. The water temperature should be cooling off by now. This is the season when fishing becomes an activity of endurance. As the fish move away from the coast, they are scarce to find, and inclement weather tries one's resilience and patience. Conversely, it is the time of the year when we catch our most elusive species.

However, the fish are everywhere, enough to catch our bag limit and fill my smokehouse! Before my eyes, climate zones are shifting and ecosystems are disrupted. Our world is interconnected and these disasters scream for global action and the mitigation of climate change.

Four years ago, we were evacuated because of our massive summer bushfires. There is only one tertiary road into this little village and it is always cut in flood or fire. We live, in this twenty-first century, as "disaster ready" humans. Escape bags, packed with torches, water, precious papers and possessions, and dog food, are ever present. We have hoses and buckets placed carefully at strategic points in case we are trapped. A constant question running through our minds through autumn and winter is, "When are they going to do some controlled burning?" Ours is a decade of high anxiety.

## Chapter 40

Puberty hit Simon's heart with a suddenness that raised problems of geography.

As in most advanced countries, there is a massive difference between the services that can be accessed when you live away from a city. We were a five-hour drive from the city. No local doctors had the expertise, nor wanted him as a patient, and after a few years of scary episodes, he was put on the heart donor list once he became eighteen and could be treated at an adult hospital. We were assured that he would be first in line for surgery if a necessity arose and that a helicopter flight could be arranged. This took a great load off my mind. Throughout his teens and twenties, the insufficiencies of that organ curtailed the life of a normal youth. No partying, alcohol, or soft drinks. No take-away food. He required about eleven hours' sleep a night.

The most dangerous activity was when he decided to try and do his Surf Lifesaving bronze medallion. This involved swimming while towing a rescue device out to a drowning swimmer and bringing them back to shore. I had notified NSW Surf Lifesaving, alerting them to the need for extra precautions. That had been promised; however, communications failed, the weather turned bad, the currents and waves became dangerous, yet he was allowed to try. I was at my parents' house waiting when three men carried Simon up to our front door saying, "We think he collapsed."

The exertion had been too much and his heart rate was down to twenty-seven beats a minute. He was eighteen, and we had been through so many emergencies I felt we might manage this without calling an ambulance. I stand by the parental decisions that I made but, as I look back, I amaze myself that I had such confidence and total faith that he would not die. He lay at my mother's house for three days just resting and eating our family's cure-all: chicken soup and fresh bread. Then life resumed once more. He had to promise not to try the Surf Lifesaving. I believe that Simon's success was because I had him when I was twenty-one and quite naïve and stupid about life. I was not wise. I had hope.

Whenever I find myself in a strange place having a bad panic attack, his phone is the one on speed dial. His calm and practical concern, his utter love, goes rushing into my ears as he talks to me. 'You are breathing, Mother. How do I know? Because we are talking. I can hear you. Look in your purse for your tablets. How about you try just a half one because I can hear you are slowing down, Mother. Take some more slow deep breaths. Slow exhale, Mother! There. That's better. Now go and make yourself a cup of tea and ring me if you need me again.' How fortunate I am!

The discipline that I had instilled in his young self has served him well. He had been denied sugar, soft drinks, packet or frozen food, as well as by necessity missing out on parties, pub crawls, and backyard barbecues. All meals are made from scratch. Further to that, he is faithful to exercise and diet and, while he is often attached to electronic heart testing equipment, he lives the best life possible.

Both of my sons absorbed the pattern of my life. They need the heave of the mighty ocean pounding its energy on clean, shell-strewn sand for their sanity and health. We are coastal people needing the pall of gulls and lonely gnarled headlands. I always identify with the Turlock family in Michener's great book *Chesapeake*. We find comfort on swamps, sedges, mangroves and tannin-coloured waters, too. In that biome we hunt our sweetest food of all, the mud crab!

Damian is a master crabber. To be truthful, he is my protein supplier as he gleans our food from under that ocean that Simon is on top of and I am swimming in. Damian goes under and is an exceptional skin diver with a huge lung capacity. As well, he knows where lobsters live, which crevices the abalone move to and, best of all, when the mud crabs are on the move. He is the one who stands in the freezing night catching fish, which he scales, bleeds and cleans. He then wanders around this village, yes, the same village of my childhood, and makes sure every elderly person, every lone person, gets a fish for dinner.

He inherited my ability to quieten wild animals, to sit in silence and observe, and thinks more than he speaks. We are all loners. That used to worry me. I wore guilt for the fact that a quite incomplete human adult raised them. I put them in danger. They were forever moving from house to house and country to country, but I think because I had made it into a game of life, they were not damaged. I hope not.

At the age of forty-nine, I was granted a disability pension as my breakdowns and panic attacks were continuous. Regrettably, I resigned from my career and began another chapter in my life. For the next fifteen years I became the carer and driver for my parents and addressed their every need. My siblings all lived away from the beach and were busy. I delighted in my parents' humour. As people of faith, they had no fear of dying and continued to trip, fall, or lose balance while laughing delightedly at their lot. As a result, they never broke any bone! Gradually, as they needed me, they showed a degree of respect, although I never heard a thank you from Mother. They were hale people with brilliant senses of humour and both had a zest for life as well as no ailments. This was a time when I was able to understand that my mother had no means of ever understanding me. I saw things from her perspective at last.

After a short decline in energy, my ninety-nine-year-old father died a beautiful death. He had no illness but one day whispered to me, 'Pet, I am going to stop eating. I am tired. Don't worry your mother.' He did that. Surrounded by our parish priest and family, he took his last breath in my arms as I whispered the rosary into his deaf ear. Both my boys had been at his side, Damian feeding him sweet tea from a teaspoon just before he closed his eyes. My father died peacefully in their new beach house. I remember the bewilderment on my mother's face. "Mother, what did you expect was going to happen?"

"Oh, Lina! I thought that the next step would be to buy a wheelchair."

She had not recognised the face of death or even the constancy of our parish priest who adored my father, came every day to say a bedroom mass for us, and considered him a saint the moment he took his last breath. My humble father, so shy he always nearly missed getting communion because he needed to get his courage up to go down the aisle, had the biggest funeral the town had seen, with even the choir loft overfull. Sometimes I am scared that no one will come and mourn me beside my two boys. I have cast no shadow.

Perhaps I had been protecting my quiet father from the reality of my trauma-induced panic attacks, because after he died and was buried, I sought help from the Church. Australia, at the time, was clamouring for a Royal Commission into child clerical sexual abuse to be held, and as well, there was a Special Inquiry into the Sexual Abuse by Clergy in the Maitland-Newcastle diocese. This was my diocese. At first, I took my courage and pride in my hands and went to speak to our parish priest, saying that I needed help, that my entire life had been coloured by the five years of abuse and assault. He said that he would get back to me. However, it took a year before he came to me with a phone number to call. I became a witness.

When I tried to tell my mother of the priest's abuse she would not listen and even on the night before she died, as I tucked her into bed, she glared at me with those brilliant blue eyes and said, firm-lipped "Don't you drag our name into that Royal Commission. I'll never forgive you!" She lived seven years after Father had gone and died just before her one-hundred-and-second birthday, still clear-headed and determined.

## Next Foot Forward

The headlines in all our newspapers screamed constantly of "Sexual abuse in the Catholic Church." I felt that the Church should respond in some way. I designed and planned an audio-visual event, 'An Atonement', with the help and financial support of the bishop. A committee was formed and I had carte blanche from the bishop, so all the meetings were held at my house as I find it difficult to leave my house. I recorded and planned the "response" from start to finish as I really wanted to show the average Australian that we were not ashamed to go public. By then it was obvious that the Church hierarchy did not have a clue how to apologise to the public in general.

On Friday September 2017, "The Atonement. Lina's Project" took place to a packed house in Newcastle City Hall. For the following two weeks, with city council approval, my project was displayed each night by being projected onto the walls of the cathedral. An impressive sight.

"Lina's Project" can be accessed on YouTube. Note, there is a trigger warning. I exposed the face of every proven paedophile priest and other clergy. When the Inquiry was published in hard form, my art decorated the front and back pages.

I was criticised for not attending. It is hard for people who listen but do not hear, and read but do not see, to understand that the result of my complex PTSD is that I am a prisoner in my own safe place. Of course I could not attend. I have been nowhere for thirty-five years, although I feel that I might be able to if one of my sons accompanied me.

The result of being a witness and going public was that I was able to access any mental health practitioners at the Church's expense. Eventually, I teamed up with a psychiatrist who suited me perfectly. Because I had not been treated for over fifty years, and each trauma seemed to catapult me into another one, causing me to be "complex," I am now hard-wired to anxiety and hypervigilance. I have a contact whom I can call upon when things roil my soul. My psychiatrist, aware of my sensitivity, assessed me carefully on various medications and I can now self-medicate.

These thoughts glide through my mind as I crouch down and peer into the steely surface of the lagoon. Light dances through the sedges and reeds like shards of broken glass. Disturbed water birds float skyward like a cloud of chaff. I have been watching a lost or gypsy pelican chase her shadow across the bright surface of the ocean. Every now and then, she pleats into a ripple on the surface. Those web-footed legs stretch out for elegant braking. Beside me, Pippi, my rescued female Italian greyhound, sticks her chest out, imitating fierceness. All three kilograms of her quiver as she prepares to protect me from whatever she is imagining. She resembles a tiny, skinny shoebox on long extended legs. She might be a guardian angel in a soft grey-and-white speckled suit.

The wind blows through my teeth. Gazing out to the choppy horizon, I think of life. You dive down. The wave blots out the sky, its lip already falling. You pass your own gentle bubbles as you sink into the billowing blue for a moment, drifting in silence. That is life.

How formidable I had been in those two decades of my life!

**Next Foot Forward**

# Chapter 41

Yesterday, the surf was angry in some places and diffident in others. I sat on my towel enjoying the salt in the air and the smell of decaying seaweed.

You should know that sometimes the beauty around me brings me to despair. I get a sense of not quite inhabiting my surroundings while my physical self is preened and pruned by sun, wind, salt, and responsibilities. I am inside my world, or it is in me.

Little seabirds, terns, hover, suspended, floating as rudderless as the unfettered memories of my mind. Storm winds creep low from the horizon, ambushing the gulls. They bounce on the air gently, as suspended as a child's mobile wafting above his crib. In unison, they move like a clutch of shredded coconut, gleeful in the inky sky.

I am left with motes of feather somewhere deep within the soul of the body that stands bereft and lonely, damply insecure of love and life once more.

"No good swimming there, lady." He stood before me, hands on hips, shaking his head like a wise old man. I had not met this local before, so I settled in to hear his opinion of life and my beach.

"It's the rip! See there? Dad says that when the top water swirls white like that, it's always a rip. High tide, too."

A skinny brown finger pointed towards the rocks.

I nodded.

"On the low," he continued, "those rocks out there are uncovered. See the big one like an elephant lying down? That's the place for abs at low tide." Abalone, abs, are molluscs, gastropods that have a fleshy foot holding them tightly to crevasses. I got up to stroll and told him that for three years I had owned the only abalone licence on this mid-north coast.

"You lived here all your life?" asked that sun-browned little face.

"All my life except for about ten years ago when my sons were about your age."

He accompanied me, pointing out the gulls circling low over the water, running ahead to investigate pieces of washed-up seaweed and shells, talking all the while.

I felt he was what I had once been, alive, attuned to nature's nuances, friendly on this piece of coast. I wondered why it was so easy for me to communicate with children, yet be bereft of adult friendship. Our wide brown feet trod firmly on the wet sand; our footprints glistened, then slowly disappeared. I watched his small, grave face as we continued to talk about diving, surfing, fishing, and the magic of the ocean. The sun slid behind a large thundercloud, and he stopped, cocking his head, listening to sounds I could not hear.

"I must go now, lady. There's a southerly blow coming and I'll have to help Dad in the yard. Bye."

He headed back the way we had come, running against the wind that I could now hear.

"There is a bluebird in my heart that wants to get out, but I am too tough for him" is a sentence written by Balzac, whom I greatly admire. I believe that bluebird struggled within my heart until various misfortunes turned that bird into a peregrine falcon of far superior strength than my toughness. Nature and its glories overtook my heart, fed my spirit, and grew in me a sense of marvellousness.

A willy-wagtail is chittering and flashing itself around my feet, searching for tiny insects. Truly, he flicks and floats like a wafting bushfire ember, then takes shape, bringing my attention back to

## Next Foot Forward

this beautiful day in March when the mullet are preparing to run. I know because the wind has turned and Easter is nearly upon us. Birdsong and happiness split the air as the world says goodbye to summer. This is a bounteous place. A place pleading to tell a secret, one involving gravity and latitude, salinity and atmosphere. The summer rains are finished, and the mullet are coming.

From the backwaters of creeks and lakes, rivers and estuaries, flows this silver stream, with twitches of fins and twists of tails. In every year of my life, this ancient rite has occurred. Year after year, the dance of silver is refined until the choreography is more heart-stopping than any recollection, any act of love, any prayer granted. Lakes and rivers and all waterways take colour as the weeks of summer rain cease, browns and greys, greens and umbers, as the salt water becomes brackish. The air smells of mudflats and leaf litter, of an eternity.

Shoals of mullet have been growing quietly and undisturbed in the safety of the waterways. It is time. The collective culture of this species now shows its willingness to pit itself against life. If you are lucky, your eyes will be filled with silver. This is the time of dreams, of magic, a time of waiting and remembering the laughs of years gone by. Mullet, the humblest of fish! They come determined to reach the open seas.

A stream of solid silver makes its way out into the oceans all along Australia's east coast shorelines, a marine Milky Way. A stream so solid you could stride across it in heavy boots or tap shoes. Wreaths of silver scales wash upon the shores while this monster flash of living light makes its own music as it snakes into the bay. The urgency to leave one phase of life and pursue the next is a statement, a lesson to all of us. These strips of mercury must mate only in the open sea. They fill the day with their light and endless reflections, and the following morning we find shimmering, glistening waves of silver scales washed up, abandoned like clothes no longer needed, jewels spilt on the sand.

www.ingramcontent.com/pod-product-compliance
Lightning Source LLC
Chambersburg PA
CBHW052032070526
44584CB00016B/2005